THE COMPLETE BEGINNER'S

BUILD A WEB SITE IN 24 HOURS

WORKS ON ANY COMPUTER

- ◆ **Learn HTML step-by-step**
- ◆ **Create slick, speedy graphics**
- ◆ **Add links, lists, tables and more**
- ◆ **Get your site online and promote it**

TELL THE WORLD ABOUT YOURSELF, YOUR FAMILY, CLUB, WHATEVER!

Published by Paragon Publishing Ltd
Paragon House, St Peter's Road,
Bournemouth, UK BH1 2JS
Tel: 01202 299900
Fax: 01202 299955
http://www.paragon.co.uk

All rights reserved. No part of this publication may be reproduced, stored in a retrieval system, or transmitted in any form whatsoever without the written consent of the publishers. This book may not be lent, re-sold hired out or otherwise disposed of by way of trade in any form of binding or cover other than that in which it is published.

While every effort has been made to ensure that the information contained in **Build A Web Site in 24 Hours** is accurate, Paragon Publishing Ltd makes no warranty, either expressed or implied, as to its quality, performance, merchantability or fitness for any purpose.

Managing Editor: Geoff Harris – geoffh@paragon.co.uk
Editor: Mark Newman – mnewman@paragon.co.uk
Production Editor: Jo Cole – pixie@paragon.co.uk
Technical Editor & Author: James Seabright – james@paragon.co.uk
Designers: Ross Andrews, Andy Hope
Printed by: Caledonian International Book Manufacturing Ltd
Published by: Paragon Publishing Ltd

CONTENTS

CHAPTER 1	*A **MASTERPLAN IN THE MAKING***	07
CHAPTER 2	***SOFTWARE SOLUTIONS***	17

BEGINNER

CHAPTER 3	***BACK TO BASICS***	27
CHAPTER 4	***CONTENT CREATION***	37
CHAPTER 5	***PAINTING BY NUMBERS***	47
CHAPTER 6	***LISTS-U-LIKE***	57
CHAPTER 7	***FINISHING TOUCHES***	67
CHAPTER 8	***SOURCE CODE ANALYSIS***	77
CHAPTER 9	***GETTING IT ONLINE***	87
CHAPTER 10	***ON THE UPLOAD***	97

INTERMEDIATE

CHAPTER 11	***TEXTUAL INTERCOURSE***	107
CHAPTER 12	***ENDLESS ENTITIES***	117
CHAPTER 13	***STYLESHEETS MADE SIMPLE***	127
CHAPTER 14	***YOU'VE BEEN FRAMED***	137
CHAPTER 15	***FORM WITH FUNCTION***	147
CHAPTER 16	***TABLES***	157
CHAPTER 17	***PREPARING GRAPHICS***	167

ADVANCED

CHAPTER 18	***IMAGEMAPS***	177
CHAPTER 19	***SCRIPTING SENSATION***	187
CHAPTER 20	***SOUNDING OFF***	197
CHAPTER 21	***BEEFED-UP BROWSER***	207
CHAPTER 22	***PLUG-IN POWER***	217
CHAPTER 23	***GET READY FOR THE ROBOTS!***	227
CHAPTER 24	***GET NOTICED***	237
APPENDIX	***32 TOP TIPS/105 HOT SITES***	247

Practical Internet
EVERY ISSUE SAVES YOU TIME, MONEY & HASSLE
GETTING ONLINE CHEAPER, FASTER AND EASIER
HOW TO POWER UP YOUR PC!
WHICH ISP OFFERS THE BEST TECH SUPPORT?
ISPs tested
Beat Net RAGE!
WHO'LL SORT YOU OUT?
SASSY SOFTWARE
Daft downloads to bring a little humour to your PC
PLUS: BEATING VIRUSES • SELLING SEX • BRAND NEW BROWSERS
FIX IT YOURSELF!
How to sort out Net hassles without calling tech support
ON THE CD
Top Net software
Plus: Over 40 free
REVEALED – THE FASTEST WAYS OF GETTING ON THE INTERNET
FASTER THAN 56k
WARP-SPEED
ON THE CD
Top Net software:
Inside: See what ev
BE AN ONLINE SEX GOD • LAST MINUTE HOLIDAY BARGAINS
VIRUS TIMEBOMB
Protect your PC from the Web's worst infections
ON THE NEW LOOK CD
TOP NET SOFTWARE:
• Millennium bug testes
• Virus detection software
• Latest IE5 and Communicator
• Net programs you simply must have
• Free Net access from eight ISPs
No Disc?
WIN!
Hit count heaven
Ten surefire tips for driving visitors to your Web site – as used by the experts
The hippest MP3s for free!
We track down the Net's very best music downloads
Plus: Free ISPs tested & compared • Earn money from your site

GET ONLINE
CHEAPER, FASTER AND EASIER

Practical Internet is the magazine that skips the hype and gets straight down to explaining, in plain English, how to get the best out of the Net without drowning in the trash. Every month, *Practical Internet* is crammed with features, reviews and advice on everything of interest to the dial-up user. So whether you want to squeeze more speed from your modem, cut your phone costs, get to grips with email, the Web and newsgroups, or avoid paying for calls to your technical support line, *Practical Internet* is all you need.

For more information turn to page 122 in the magazine or call **01202 200200**

Published by Paragon Publishing Ltd
Paragon House, St Peter's Road,
Bournemouth, UK, BH1 2JS
Tel: 01202 299900
Fax: 01202 299955
http://www.paragon.co.uk

CHAPTER 01

A MASTERPLAN IN THE MAKING

MASTERPLAN IN THE MAKING

Planning

This is the all-important first step in Web page creation. If you just dive in, chances are your site will end up a disjointed, unstructured mess – a recipe for disaster that will not win favour on the Web.

This chapter provides a fail-safe checklist of things to consider before you start to build your pages. Once you've achieved this, you are ready to begin – either by using one of the Web editing software packages recommended in Chapter Two, or by following the full HTML tutorial that starts in Chapter Three.

Planning makes perfect: Yahoo! grew to be the incredible success it is today thanks to a well thought-out plan developed by its youthful founders, Jerry Yang and David Filo

MASTERPLAN IN THE MAKING

Web space

There is little point in creating a site until you have secured somewhere to put it. Although you won't use your Web space until the project is completed, this is an essential first step – especially so that you know the address (URL) of your pages during the design stage.

Take a look at the listing of free Web space providers in Chapter Seven to get some ideas together. Alternatively, check whether your ISP provides any free Web space itself – this is often a better way of doing things, as ISP-hosted pages tend to be advert-free and often provide a customised sub-domain name like **http://www.mypages.freeserve.co.uk**.

Track down some free Web space using this listing service at http://freeweblist.freeservers.com/

---

move your site to Freeservers TODAY!!!

FREE WEB PAGES | Free Stats/Counter | Submit Your URL

The Free-Webpage Listing

Add moneymaking content to your site for free!

Making your presence felt on the World Wide Web need not be an expensive venture. If your looking to make yourself or your special interest known to the world or to give your company an international exposure you can get webspace for free. Keep in mind that some webspace providers may require you to host their banner or have pop-up windows in exchange for the service they provide while others may not let you put any kind of paid advertising on your site.

Under 3MB
3MB to 10MB
Over 10MB

Free E-mail Providers
Free Website Resources
Free newsletters
Free Associate Programs
Free Classifieds
Email the webmaster

Any way you take it having a free website can be just as rewarding as paying top dollar with some providers. You should list out your requirements before starting your search and then find the one that best fits your needs by comparing your list to the tables of providers on this website.

This list is by no means finished as there are lots of free website providers out there that I have never heard about. If you have any suggestions or additions to the list you can email them to the webmaster at **Cm103@netscape.net**.

MASTERPLAN IN THE MAKING

Software

There's more than one way to make a Web page. The main decision you have to make is whether to write the HTML code yourself, or to use a Web editing program to do this automatically – some of the more popular packages are covered in Chapter Two. Don't be afraid to follow the manual coding route – the tutorial that starts in Chapter Three covers the absolute basics. Manually creating pages also gives far superior control over the final outcome.

If you decide to code the HTML yourself, then Windows Notepad or MacOS SimpleText do the job. You'll also need to use other programs such as graphics editors and FTP software. Paint Shop Pro (**http://www.jasc.com**) and CuteFTP (**http://www.cuteftp.com**) both come highly recommended.

Software house JASC provides the ever-popular PaintShop Pro graphics package, which is available for a 30-day free trial from http://www.jasc.com/

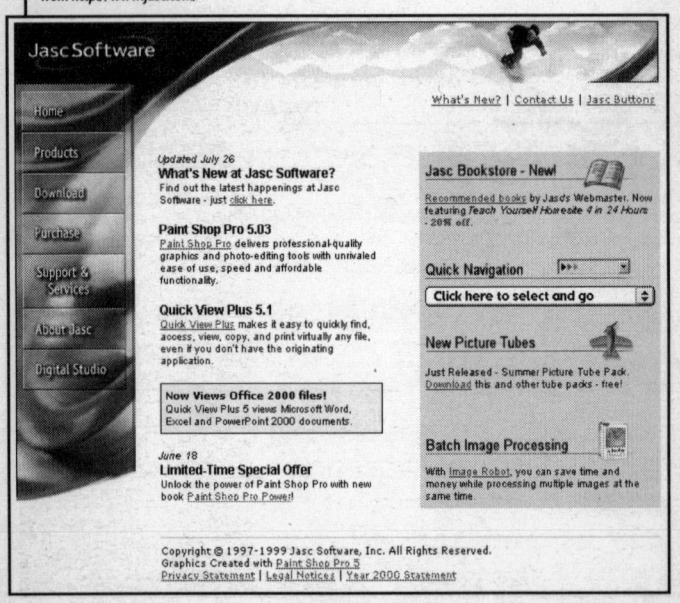

MASTERPLAN IN THE MAKING

Concept and structure
Think of a working title and key message or concept that the site is aiming to convey. When you get into difficult decision-making territory, you can refer back to these starting points to help decide what will best suit the required purpose. It doesn't matter if the title is something simple like John Jacobs' Home Page – the important thing is that you have a firm aim in mind.

This is closely linked to the question of how the material of your Web site is going to be organised. Is it small enough to fit on one page, or do you need lots of categories and index pages to bring it all into a sensible order? Sketch out a diagram to work out the answers to these questions.

Take a look at some of the great sites listed at http://cool.infi.net/ to get some ideas about how your site might stand out from the crowd

Cool Site of the Day
THE ORIGINAL
TODAY'S COOL SITE

CDs, DVDs AND VIDEOS ON SALE!
All new releases at **Total E** are on sale and shipping is only 99¢ for a limited time! Order **now** and get **$5 off** your purchase of $25 or more in addition to the sale price!!

Cool Zones
Cool Activism
Cool AudioVideo
Cool Books
Cool Cars
Cool Community
Cool Fashion
Cool Free Stuff
Cool Gifts
Cool Jobs
Cool Learning
Cool Money
Cool Movies
Cool Music
Cool News

MASTERPLAN IN THE MAKING

Look and feel This is closely related to the previous point and how structure is translated into a navigation system using HTML. You need to think about whether frames will be required and if so, how they will be designed. If not, think of a consistent means of navigation to help users find their way around. This links to the question of what your site is going to look like. This is often misinterpreted in terms of graphic files alone, which is unduly restrictive. Consider background, text and link colours, along with font faces and design 'house style.' For example, what configuration of horizontal rule will be used throughout? What font size should be used for headlines? Will text be left-aligned or centred? Make decisions, and stay consistent throughout the site design.

Get some hints on how to make your graphic design bandwidth-efficient by visiting http://www.infohiway.com/faster/index.html

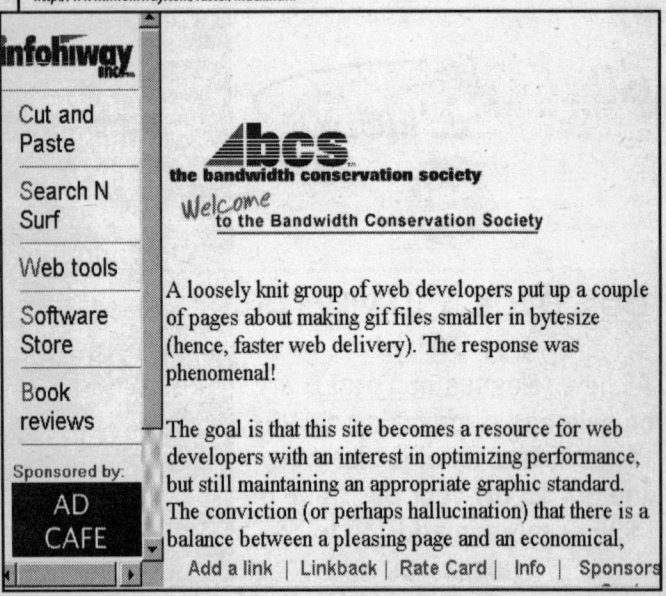

---

infohiway inc.

- Cut and Paste
- Search N Surf
- Web tools
- Software Store
- Book reviews

Sponsored by:
AD CAFE

bcs
the bandwidth conservation society

Welcome to the Bandwidth Conservation Society

A loosely knit group of web developers put up a couple of pages about making gif files smaller in bytesize (hence, faster web delivery). The response was phenomenal!

The goal is that this site becomes a resource for web developers with an interest in optimizing performance, but still maintaining an appropriate graphic standard. The conviction (or perhaps hallucination) that there is a balance between a pleasing page and an economical,

Add a link | Linkback | Rate Card | Info | Sponsors

MASTERPLAN IN THE MAKING

Technologies Consider whether it is necessary to use any special technologies to convey your site's message. Rule out the use of such features if the only reason you can think of is to show off your skill in HTML. This school of Web design, where 'eye candy' is king, never wins friends among the vast majority of users who are connected to the Net via relatively slow modem links.

If extra technologies are used, consider whether this is going to work with your Web space provider (some limit the use of RealAudio, for example). Also, think about whether you will be frustrating visitors by requiring them to download a plug-in.

Find out all you need to know about advanced Web technologies by visiting http://www.htmlgoodies.com/

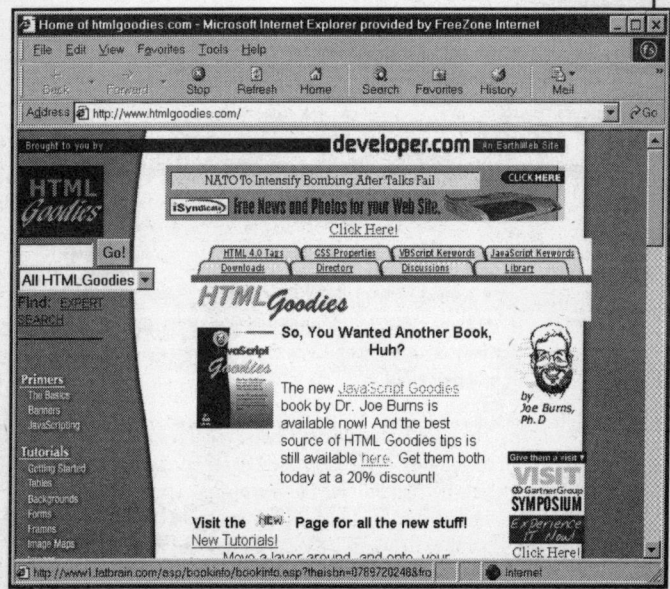

MASTERPLAN IN THE MAKING

Interactivity
Web sites aren't supposed to be a one-way means of communication. Think of how you can encourage interactivity on your site, even if it is only by including a guestbook or strawpoll survey on the front page. More ambitious users might want discussion or chat groups.

All of these resources can be found free on the Net and a great place to start is **http://www.free.com**. It's also a good idea to keep an eye on *Practical Internet's* Home Improvement section, where free Web resources are featured each issue.

Add a chat room or bulletin board to your site completely free of charge at http://www.beseen.com/

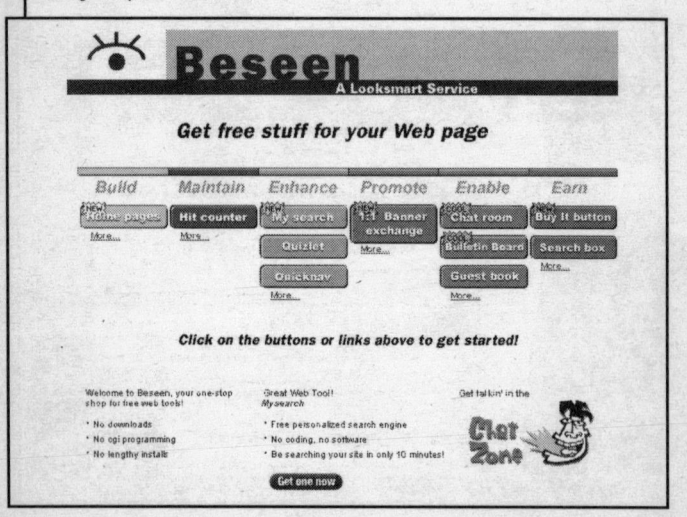

MASTERPLAN IN THE MAKING

Timescale
With the fluidity of Web site publishing, it is very easy to just keep working on your pages and never finish them. Be firm with yourself and set a realistic deadline that you will be able to keep.

Think about how many pages there are to make and how many graphics you need to create for each one. Then you should be able to figure out a reasonable timescale depending on your proficiency level with HTML.

As well as keeping a personal perspective on the timescale of your project, activate your site with Swatch's Internet Time at http://www.swatch.com/internettime/beatnik_fs_time.html

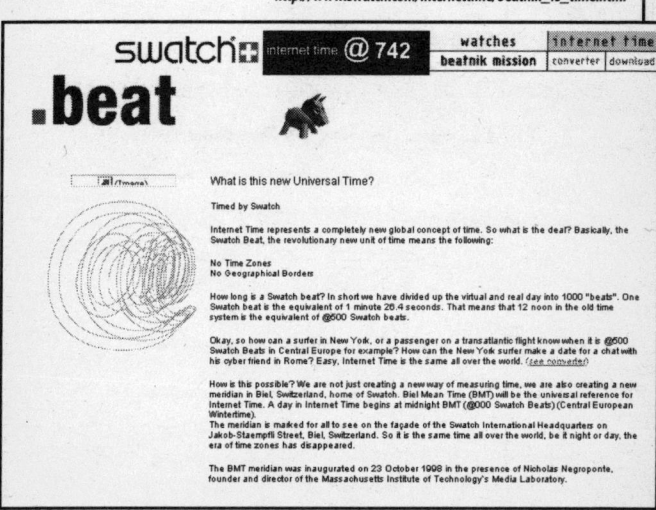

---

swatch internet time @ 742 | watches | internet time
beatnik mission | converter | download

.beat

What is this new Universal Time?

Timed by Swatch

Internet Time represents a completely new global concept of time. So what is the deal? Basically, the Swatch Beat, the revolutionary new unit of time means the following:

No Time Zones
No Geographical Borders

How long is a Swatch beat? In short we have divided up the virtual and real day into 1000 "beats". One Swatch beat is the equivalent of 1 minute 26.4 seconds. That means that 12 noon in the old time system is the equivalent of @500 Swatch beats.

Okay, so how can a surfer in New York, or a passenger on a transatlantic flight know when it is @500 Swatch Beats in Central Europe for example? How can the New York surfer make a date for a chat with his cyber friend in Rome? Easy, Internet Time is the same all over the world. (see converter)

How is this possible? We are not just creating a new way of measuring time, we are also creating a new meridian in Biel, Switzerland, home of Swatch. Biel Mean Time (BMT) will be the universal reference for Internet Time. A day in Internet Time begins at midnight BMT (@000 Swatch Beats) (Central European Wintertime).
The meridian is marked for all to see on the façade of the Swatch International Headquarters on Jakob-Staempfli Street, Biel, Switzerland. So it is the same time all over the world, be it night or day, the era of time zones has disappeared.

The BMT meridian was inaugurated on 23 October 1998 in the presence of Nicholas Negroponte, founder and director of the Massachusetts Institute of Technology's Media Laboratory.

CHAPTER 02

SOFTWARE SOLUTIONS

SOFTWARE SOLUTIONS

The bulk of this book's tutorials relate to the hand coding of HTML, although it is also possible to create Web pages using software which generates all the HTML for you. Although this leaves the user with less control than if they were writing the HTML themselves, it can be a quicker and easier route to a home page. For the benefit of any readers interested in using this sort of software, a selection of available packages appears over the next few pages, together with details of how to try them out for free.

All of the latest free trial versions of Web editing software are available at http://www.download.com – but they can be incredibly large downloads, so it's often better to look out for them on the cover CD of Practical Internet

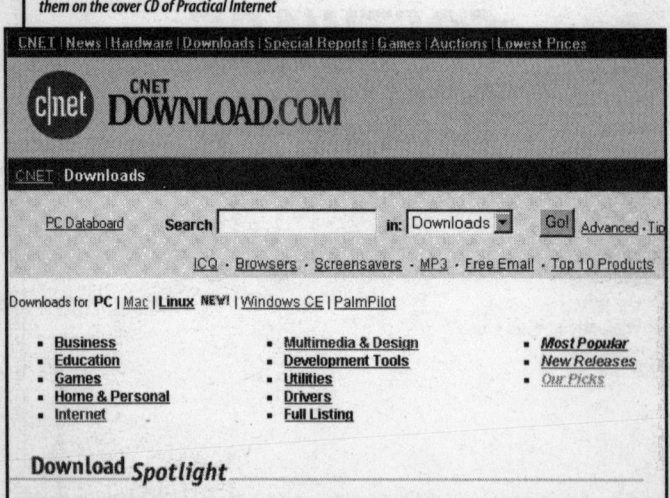

SOFTWARE SOLUTIONS

Adobe PageMill 3.0

For a product from publishing pioneer Adobe, this package is beginning to look a little jaded, even alongside those in a similar price range. PageMill is certainly very simple to get to grips with – the drag-and-drop editing is very nifty. There are some handy features like automatic recognition of graphic files being updated, but PageMill lacks the high-end features that Filemaker has put into the latest HomePage and fails to really benefit from the features poached from its ex-sister product SiteMill. Overall, a fairly harmless but somewhat confused budget offering.

Program: Adobe PageMill 3.0
URL: http://www.adobe.com
Price: £69 (excl. VAT)
Free trial: 15 days, downloadable from Web site
Mac version available

Adobe Home | Map | Index
News | Products | Solutions | Studio | Support

presenting **Adobe PageMill 3.0**
Easily Create and Manage Pages for the Web

solutions

- Easily build Web pages
- Add dazzling images and sounds
- Efficiently maintain your entire site

SOFTWARE SOLUTIONS

Allaire HomeSite 4.0

HomeSite is a particular favourite among Web editing packages, mainly because it encourages the user to get to grips with the delights of HTML. At the same time, it does make it easy for beginners to get pages on the Net with the minimum of fuss. This side of things has especially been improved with the introduction of new features in version four – there are visual layout tools at last! The major problem with HomeSite is its tight integration with Internet Explorer. Although this is impressive, it effectively discourages checking pages with Netscape before putting them on the Web.

Program: Allaire HomeSite 4.0
URL: http://www.allaire.com
Price: £65 (excl. VAT)
Free trial: 30 days, downloadable from http://www.allaire.com/download

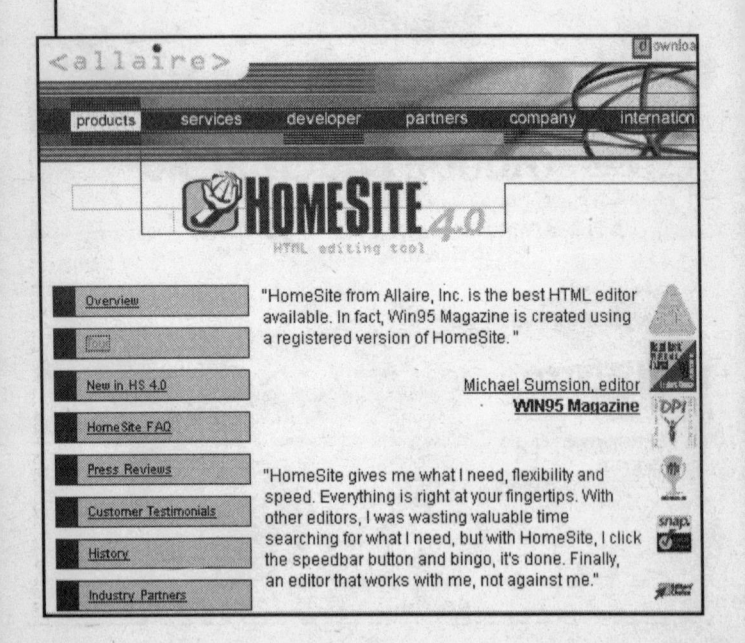

"HomeSite from Allaire, Inc. is the best HTML editor available. In fact, Win95 Magazine is created using a registered version of HomeSite."

Michael Sumsion, editor
WIN95 Magazine

"HomeSite gives me what I need, flexibility and speed. Everything is right at your fingertips. With other editors, I was wasting valuable time searching for what I need, but with HomeSite, I click the speedbar button and bingo, it's done. Finally, an editor that works with me, not against me."

SOFTWARE SOLUTIONS

Filemaker HomePage 3.0

With the introduction of database integration through Filemaker Pro in version three, HomePage has taken on something of a dual personality. On the one hand, there is the incredibly easy-to-use Web editing package in the sturdy mould of ClarisWorks. Beginners will take a shine to the familiar interface and revel in the range of features and options available. On the other hand, HomePage is the most sophisticated and difficult package to grasp of the lot. In what seems to have been a desperate rush to introduce a window to Filemaker and therefore dynamic database pages, you will find some incredibly high-end features that will never be of any use to most readers.

Program:	Claris HomePage 3.0
URL:	http://www.filemaker.com
Price:	£69 (excl. VAT)
Free trial:	30 days, downloadable from Web site
	Mac version available

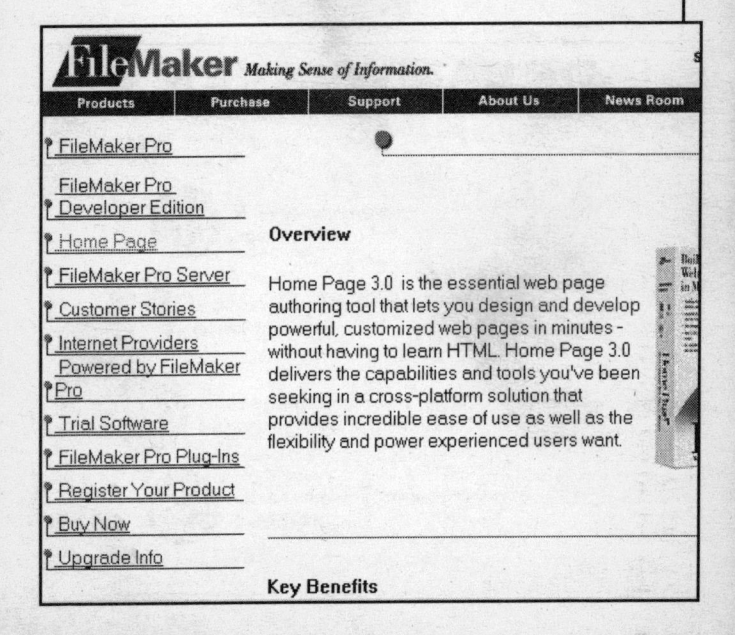

FileMaker *Making Sense of Information.*

| Products | Purchase | Support | About Us | News Room |

- FileMaker Pro
- FileMaker Pro Developer Edition
- Home Page
- FileMaker Pro Server
- Customer Stories
- Internet Providers Powered by FileMaker Pro
- Trial Software
- FileMaker Pro Plug-Ins
- Register Your Product
- Buy Now
- Upgrade Info

Overview

Home Page 3.0 is the essential web page authoring tool that lets you design and develop powerful, customized web pages in minutes - without having to learn HTML. Home Page 3.0 delivers the capabilities and tools you've been seeking in a cross-platform solution that provides incredible ease of use as well as the flexibility and power experienced users want.

Key Benefits

Macromedia Dreamweaver 2

This package is one of the two expensive items listed here, costing over £200. The reason for this is that Dreamweaver is an incredibly well-accomplished powerhouse of Web publishing, with a very accurate rendition of HTML and a particular emphasis on dynamic features, graphics and plug-ins. As a fan of BBEdit, I have taken a particular liking to the 'parallel editing' where you can tinker with HTML in the text editor and have the changes automatically rendered in the Dreamweaver preview window. If you are serious about using the latest Web technologies, then this is, without doubt, the product of choice. Certainly it is worthwhile to take a look at the free trial and see what you think.

Program:	Macromedia Dreamweaver 2
URL:	http://www.dreamweaver.com
Price:	£229 (excl. VAT)
Free trial:	30 days, downloadable from Web site
	Mac version available

DREAMWEAVER 2
the solution for professional web site design and production

- get dreamweaver 2 free trial version
- download free extensions to dreamweaver
- dreamweaver/fireworks hands-on-training. sign up now!
- dreamweaver/fireworks studio only $399

SOFTWARE SOLUTIONS

Microsoft FrontPage 2000

As would be expected from a Microsoft product, FrontPage is irrevocably dedicated to the Internet Explorer interpretation of the HTML standard. This can mean that other Web browsers have problems accurately rendering Web pages that have been created by FrontPage. On the positive side, the software has the feel of the more expensive packages listed here, whilst retaining a fair budget pricing. Every aspect of the design of your site is catered for, including graphics and site templates through the vast selection of samples that are included. Beginners may be a little flustered by some features, such as the integrated Web server that is used to preview pages in Explorer.

Program: Microsoft FrontPage 2000
URL: http://www.microsoft.com/frontpage
Price: £99 (excl. VAT)
Free trial: 45 days

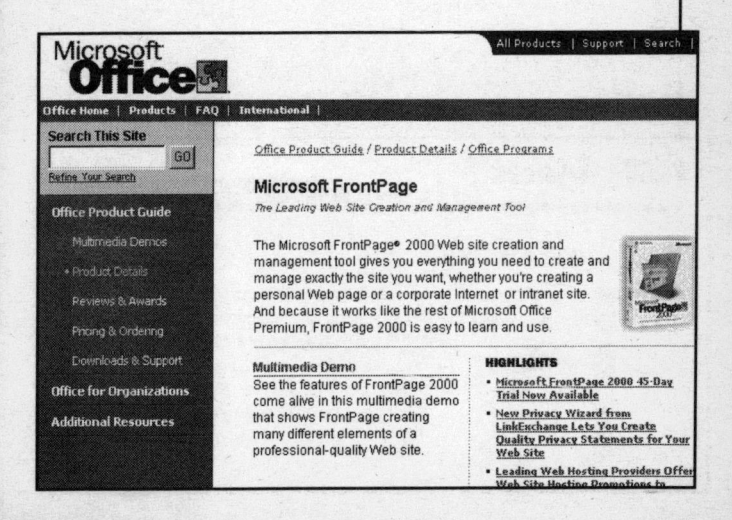

NetObjects Fusion

If you can stomach the price, then this is the Web editing package of choice for every purpose you could imagine. It is entirely possible to use NetObjects as a beginner without ever encountering difficulty, through the simple templates that are included. Alternatively, you can opt to throw yourself in at the deep end and design everything from scratch. The software encourages you to think about the capabilities of your 'target' browser and will create HTML on-the-fly to match various different browsers' specifications. Special effects can be difficult to get to grips with and you will need a big monitor to avoid drowning in a sea of floating palettes.

Program:	NetObjects Fusion 4
URL:	http://www.netobjects.com/
Price:	£165 (excl. VAT)
Free trial:	30 days, downloadable from Web site
	Mac version available

NetObjects Fusion

Whether you're building your first Web site or a site loaded with online catalogs, e-commerce, or Web applications, you'll get your business online fast with NetObjects

SOFTWARE SOLUTIONS

SoftQuad HoTMetaL Pro 5.0

This product continues to prove incredibly popular as an upgrade from the shareware version, where many people begin their Web design experiences. The interface has a feel similar to PageMill or HomeSite, although with more editing views than either of them. The 'tags on view' mode is an excellent hybrid of visual and source code editing, despite the fact that it can become difficult to see exactly what your page is going to look like when the tags disappear. However, there is little else to recommend this package above the Adobe and Claris offerings – which are both £20 cheaper.

Program: SoftQuad HoTMetaL Pro 5.0
URL: http://www.softquad.com
Price: £99 (excl. VAT)
Free trial: 30 days, downloadable from Web site

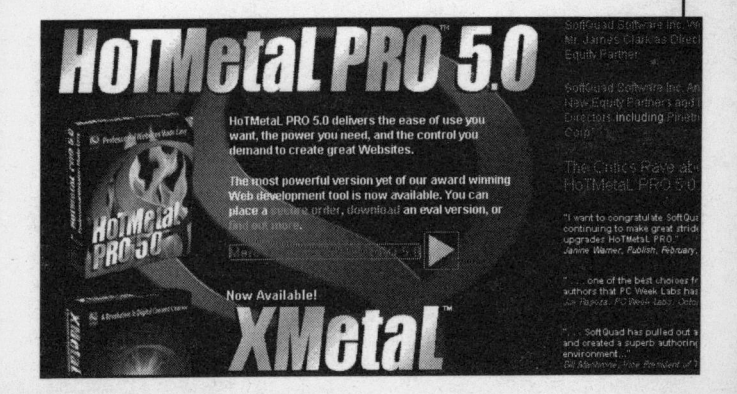

CHAPTER 03

BEGINNER: BACK TO BASICS

BEGINNER: BACK TO BASICS

Step One Contrary to popular belief, setting up your own Web page is a devilishly simple operation. Regardless of what computer you are using, you will be able to make a simple but good-looking site by following the instructions through the next nine chapters. To prove the point, we arranged for a local goat called George to do just that. You can see his comments throughout the text, and view the fruits of his farmyard labours at **http://www.paragon.co.uk/george/**. George used Windows 98 and its built-in text editor called Notepad, although there are plenty of other combinations (for example, Mac OS users can use SimpleText).

BEGINNER: BACK TO BASICS

Step Two
In case you didn't know, HTML stands for HyperText Markup Language. This means that plain text can be 'marked up' using tags and commands which enhance and change the appearance of the document when viewed using a Web browser. Anyone who has ever selected 'View source' in their Web browser will know that these tags are defined by the characters < and >. So, the tag **<P>** has a specific meaning: it tells the browser to insert a paragraph break at that point in the Web page.

The World Wide Web Consortium at http://www.w3.org/ is the home of HTML and you can find plenty of reference material about the language on its Web pages

Step Three

As well as the basic standalone HTML tags, some need to be 'ended' as well. For example, if you want to make some text appear bold, then the tag **<B>** is used. When you want the bold text to end, a **</B>** tag is needed

Not every tag actually translates into a visible feature in the Web browser window. There are certain tags that are required to divide the HTML code into clear sections. **<HTML>** and **</HTML>** should always be at the start and end of a Web page, simply to keep the browser happy.

Remember, tags don't have to be entered in capital letters, although this does make it easier to distinguish them from the rest of the HTML document.

This shows a section of the HTML code for the World Wide Web Consortium site on page 30. Don't worry - it's much easier than it looks!

```html
<h1><img alt="The World Wide Web Consortium (W3C)" height="48" width="307" src="Icons
</h1>

<h2><i>Leading the Web to its Full Potential...</i></h2>

<h2>W3C Issues Recommendation for Associating Style Sheets with XML
Documents</h2>

<P>The latest W3C Recommendation,
<a href="1999/06/REC-xml-stylesheet-19990629/">
"Associating Style Sheets with XML documents"</a>,
provides authors with an interoperable
mechanism for adding style to XML documents.
<span class="shortquote"><a href="Style/">Style sheets</a> are an
essential step in <a href="XML/">XML</a>
deployment, as without them there is no way to
define the presentation of XML documents which use new schemas,"</span> says
<strong>Tim Berners-Lee</strong>,
W3C Director. (<a href="1999/06/XMLStyle-PressRelease">Press
Release</a>, <a href="1999/06/XMLStyle-test">Testimonials</a>).

<p>Other news:</p>
<ul>
<LI><A href="Amaya/User/BinDist.html">Amaya 2.1 available
for Windows and Unix</a>
<LI><a href="TR/1999/WAI-WEBCONTENT-19990505">Web Content
Accessibility Guidelines 1.0</a> (<a
href="1999/05/WCAG-RECPressRelease">Press Release</a>, <a
href="1999/05/WCAG-REC-test">Testimonials</a>, <a
href="1999/05/WCAG-REC-fact">Fact Sheet</a>)
</ul>
```

BEGINNER: BACK TO BASICS

Step Four Launch your text editor. In Windows 95 or 98, you can find Notepad in the Start menu under Programs and Accessories. As mentioned before, every Web page needs certain tags to be recognised by a browser.

Type in the text as shown in the picture below, replacing George's title and message with your own. Remember that < and > are accessed by using the comma and full stop keys in combination with the Shift key. Also, a forward slash – **/** – is required for end tags like **</HTML>** – backslashes are not recognised by the code.

```
<HTML>

<HEAD>
<TITLE>Welcome to George the Goat's Farmyard Frolics</TITLE>
</HEAD>

<BODY>
George the Goat's Farmyard Frolics!
</BODY>

</HTML>
```

Build a Web Site in 24 Hours

Chapter 03

BEGINNER: BACK TO BASICS

Step Five
Now it is time to save your page for the first time, by selecting 'Save' from the File menu. Navigate your way to the Windows desktop, by clicking the pull-down menu at the top of the dialogue box and selecting 'Desktop' from the list. Then click on 'Create new folder.'

Now enter the name of the folder, in this case, 'george.' Change the 'Save as type' option to 'All Files' by clicking on the pull-down menu. Then type in 'index.htm' (in the File name box) as the name of your page, and then click on the 'Save' button.

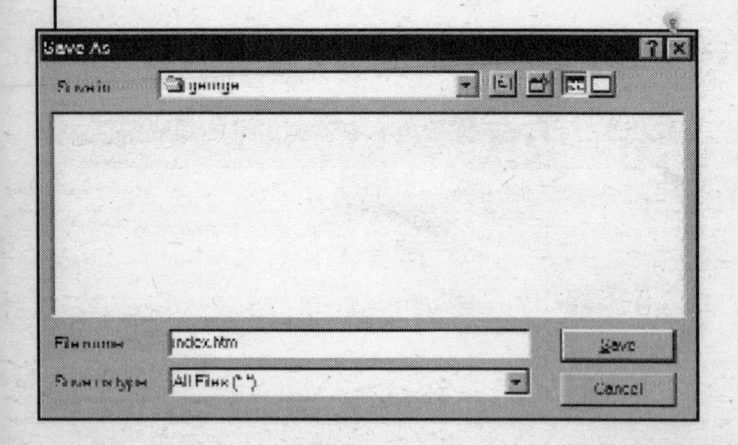

BEGINNER: BACK TO BASICS

Step Six Take a look at the page so far by launching your Web browser. Explorer users should select 'Open' from the File menu, and then click the 'Browse.' If you are using Netscape, select 'Open Page.'

Both browsers will now show a file listing. Locate and select your 'index.htm' file in this listing, and click 'Open.' Your page will then be displayed in the browser window.

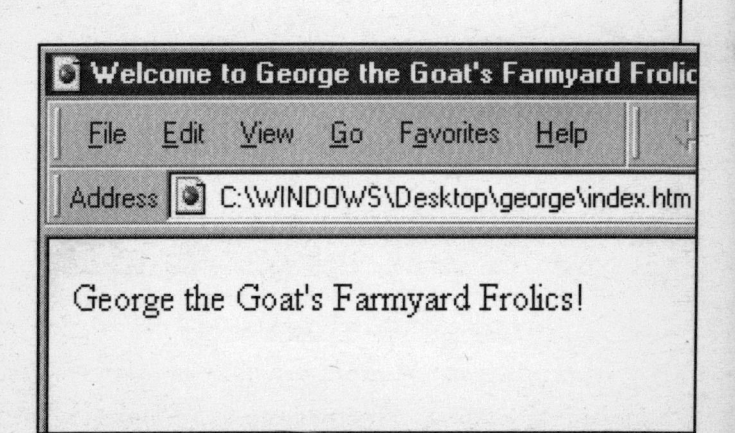

Welcome to George the Goat's Farmyard Frolic

File Edit View Go Favorites Help

Address: C:\WINDOWS\Desktop\george\index.htm

George the Goat's Farmyard Frolics!

BEGINNER: BACK TO BASICS

Step Seven
Now we'll change the look of the text a little. Switch back to your HTML code in Notepad, and move the cursor to the start of the headline in the **<BODY>** section.

Type **<CENTER><FONT SIZE="6">** before the headline, and **</FONT></CENTER>** after it. This will have the dual effect of shifting the headline to the centre of the page, and enlarging the text. Note that you must use the American spelling – 'center' – for the tag to work.

Hit 'Return' to start a fresh line, and type **<HR>**. This tag draws a line across the page, and automatically adds a paragraph break afterwards. Save the document and switch back to your browser to take a look.

BEGINNER: BACK TO BASICS

George says...

"Well that was easy. I have already got a result. I notice that the text I typed into the <TITLE> tag has appeared in the title bar of the page, and that my <BODY> text is in the main section of the window."

CHAPTER 04

BEGINNER: CONTENT CREATION

BEGINNER: CONTENT CREATION

Step One

This section will show you how to add some real text and a graphic to your page, without needing to get involved with any awkward and confusing image editing programs (although if that sounds appealing, take a look at Chapter 17).

Make sure you have your HTML file on the screen, in Notepad or whatever text editor you are using. To prepare for typing in longer amounts of text, select 'Word Wrap' from the Edit menu in Notepad.

If you're using a different text editor, then you should find a similar option is available elsewhere – although Apple's Simpletext has an automatic word wrap feature.

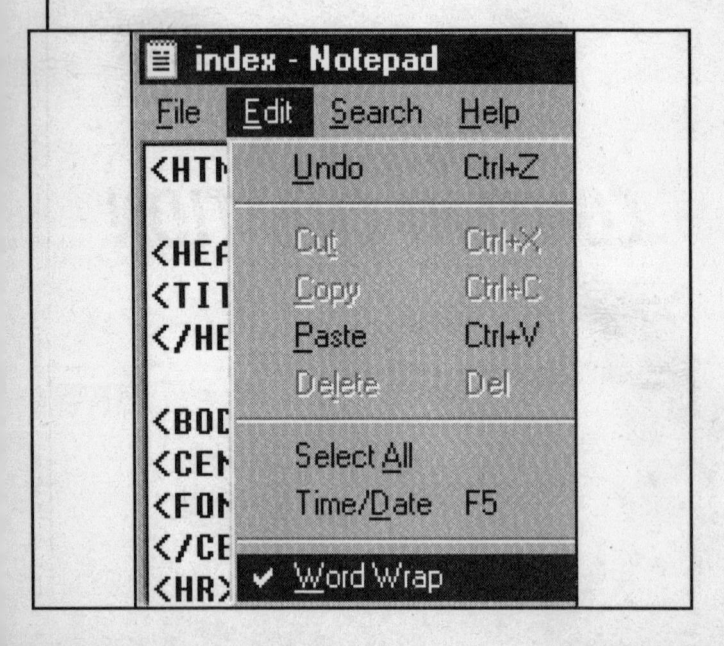

BEGINNER: CONTENT CREATION

Step Two Position the cursor after the <HR> tag, and start a new line by hitting 'Return.' Think about how you would like to introduce yourself to the world – maybe you want to say who you are, where you live and what your home page is all about.

As a general guide, do not write more than five lines of text in Notepad. Remember that paragraphs must be ended with the **<P>** tag, so make sure this concludes your introductory section. As you have done before, save the file and take a look at the result in your browser window.

George the Goat's Farmyard Frolics!

Hello there, my name is George the Goat and I have great pleasure in sharing with you my Farmyard Frolics. Contrary to the fantastical tales you may have read about farms, there is actually very little that goes on. To avoid complete boredom, I picked up a copy of Practical Internet from the local newsagent and created this page.

My farm is in a very historic part of rural England, and I enjoy cycling around the area to take beautiful photographs of the surroundings.

George says...

"I decided to introduce myself by briefly mentioning what is important to my life on the farm. I broke this into two paragraphs using the <P> tag. I also noticed that when I leave a blank line in the HTML code, this isn't shown in the browser – you can only produce blank lines with <P> tags."

BEGINNER: CONTENT CREATION

Step Three
It can take a lot of time and effort to create graphics for your Web page. For the moment, George has been kind enough to supply some graphics which you can use on your page, at **http://paragon.co.uk/george/pictures.html**.

There are instructions on that Web page about how to copy the pictures to your hard drive. Using these will save a lot of time compared with making your own and you can always go back later and slot your own designs in if you want.

BEGINNER: CONTENT CREATION

Step Four If you already have clipart images, these can also be used, provided they are in the correct format. The only formats which Web browsers can understand are GIF and JPEG – you cannot use BMP or PICT files like those created by the paint packages built in to Windows 95 and the Mac OS.

By downloading graphics from one of the free graphics sites listed at **http://www.clip-art.com/** you can be sure they are in the right format.

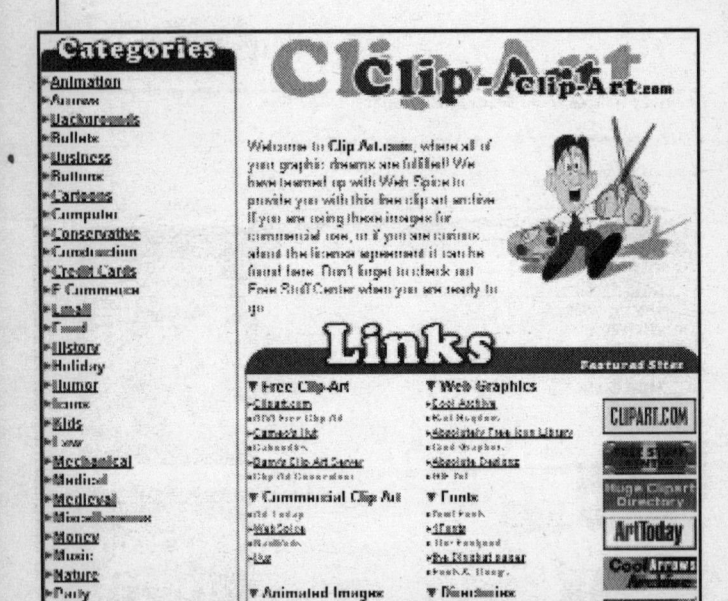

BEGINNER: CONTENT CREATION

Step Five
Now you need to get yourself a graphic to put on the page. One is plenty for the moment – the main thing is not what the picture shows, but that you get some practise including them in your page.

All the images for your Web page should be kept in a directory within the main folder. Call it 'images' and create it using the same procedure as for the main folder; when you go to save an image, simply click the 'New folder' button in the dialogue box.

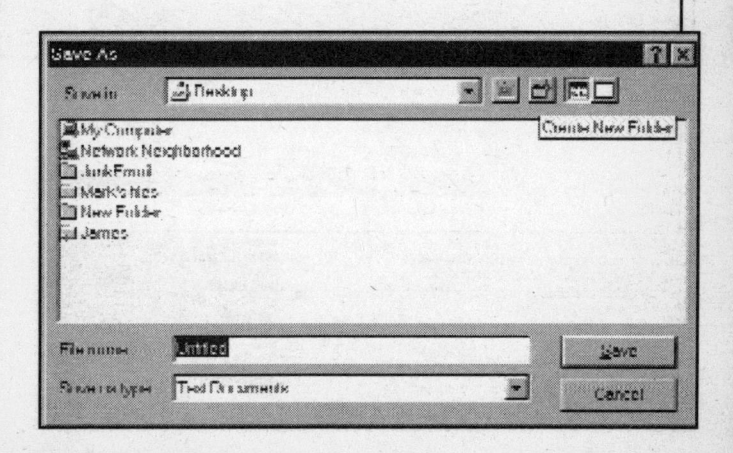

BEGINNER: CONTENT CREATION

Step Six
Return to Notepad and position the cursor at the start of the introductory paragraphs of text. Type in: **<IMG SRC="images/image.gif" ALIGN="RIGHT">** and hit the 'Return' button.

Be sure to enter the image name exactly as you saved it – for George this was 'george.gif.' This is very important, because the Web is mainly case-sensitive: GEORGE.GIF is not the same as george.gif. Save the file, and switch to your browser. Reload to see the picture in its position.

BEGINNER: *CONTENT CREATION*

George says...

"Famous at last! I've managed to get my picture to sit neatly alongside the introductory paragraph of my Web page without any problems. It's amazing how easy it is to make the Web page look good: just one line of HTML code is enough to make a picture appear wherever you want."

CHAPTER 05

BEGINNER: PAINTING BY NUMBERS

BEGINNER: PAINTING BY NUMBERS

Step One It is important to think about background colour and text colour. Choose the wrong combination and no one will be able to read your words of wisdom! It is possible to alter the colour of any element of your Web page, although there are a number of standard page elements that are easiest to configure. These include the background, text and link colours. To try out different colour combinations make a visit to **http://www.hidaho.com/colorcenter/cc.html**. This page operates by JavaScript, which means you don't have to stay online once you've loaded the page in your browser window. Don't worry if the colour codes you see here are confusing – they're explained on the next page.

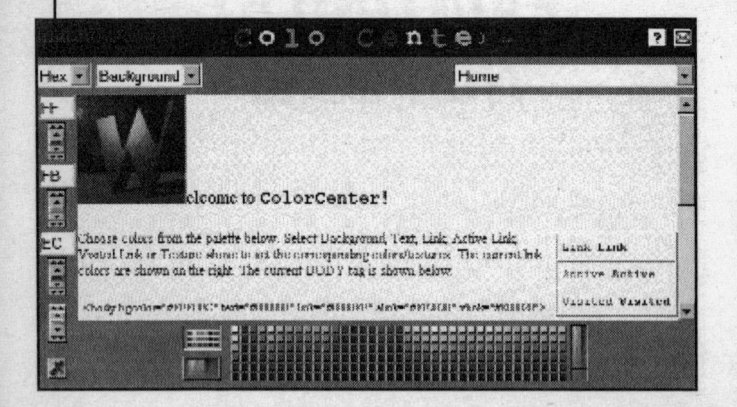

BEGINNER: PAINTING BY NUMBERS

049

<u>Step Two</u> At the moment, your page is looking decidedly monochrome. Thankfully, it is very easy to change this with a few tweaks of the HTML code. All that you need to know are the special 'colour codes' and where to use them. The colour codes are six-digit strings of letters and numbers that tell the Web browser which colour to use – for example, red is #FF0000 and white is #FFFFFF. The most commonly used 25 colour codes are listed on the swatch over the page.

These colours can be used to brighten up text, page backgrounds, link colours and many other advanced elements of page design. To change the page background colour, a BGCOLOR property is added to the BODY tag and you can change the colour of text sections using COLOR which you'll find in the FONT tag.

Visit http://www.lynda.com/hex.html to link into Lynda Weinman's excellent Web colour charts, which provide the all-important magic hex codes at a glance

<coloring web graphics>
the definitive guide to color on the web

The Browser Safe Color Palette

By Lynda Weinman

For those of you unfamiliar with my books, Designing Web Graphics.2, Deconstructing Web Graphics, Coloring Web Graphics; they go into great detail about subjects which may be

Build a Web Site in 24 Hours Chapter 05

BEGINNER: PAINTING BY NUMBERS

Step Three Take a look at the colour swatch below, and decide which colour you would like your page background to be. As you can't see the colour on this monochrome page, it's a good idea to test out a few different ones on your page to see which looks best.

Of course, it's a bad idea to choose a dark background colour as this will make text fairly unreadable (unless you change the colour of everything else to be light). Alternatively, you could always 'borrow' a colour scheme from somebody else's Web page by looking at the HTML source of their page and noting down the colour codes used in the **<BODY>** tag. Imitation, as they say, is the sincerest form of flattery...

White #FFFFFF	Black #000000	Red #FF0000	Green #00FF00	Blue #0000FF
Magenta #FF00FF	Cyan #00FFFF	Yellow #FFFF00	Aquamarine #70DB93	Dark green #2F4F2F
Light blue #C0D9D9	Light green #32CD32	Orange #E47833	Pink #BC8F8F	Summer sky #236B8E
Turquoise #ADEAEA	Violet #4F2F4F	Thistle #D8BFD8	Goldenrod #DBDB70	Maroon #8E236B
Lightest grey #DDDDDD	Lighter grey #A8A8A8	Medium grey #545454	Darker grey #454545	Darkest grey #333333

BEGINNER: PAINTING BY NUMBERS

Step Four Now that you've decided on the colour scheme, it's just a matter of incorporating this into the HTML code. The main colour codes are placed in the **<BODY>** tag of the page.

So, if you want to make the background light green (#32CD32), change the **<BODY>** tag to read **<BODY BGCOLOR="#32CD32">**. For a different colour, simply insert a different colour code instead.

If you're feeling particularly ambitious, you can also use background images by adding a **BACKGROUND="image.gif"** property to the BODY tag. When using background images, restrict yourself to a simple texture (plenty are available from the site mentioned earlier, **http://www.clip-art.com/**).

Yet another colour assistant site can be found at http://www.colormix.com/. This one helps you to increase the range of colours available for safe use in your Web browser

Step Five

Text colour can easily be changed by altering the **FONT** tag. Try this out by moving the cursor to the headline, which you entered as **<FONT SIZE="6">**. Change this to read **<FONT SIZE="6" COLOR="#0000FF">** and you will have a blue headline.

You can alter the colour of all the text on the page by changing the **BODY** tag to include a **TEXT** property. So if you want all your text to be blue, then you would add **TEXT="#0000FF"**. Try using different colours from the colour swatch shown in Step Three. Remember to use the American spelling of colour to keep Web browsers happy.

Be careful to choose a text colour that goes well with the background. In other words, yellow on white or lilac with bright green are probably best avoided

BEGINNER: PAINTING BY NUMBERS

Step Six The image below shows how Web browsers change link colours depending on whether you have already visited that link. In this example, the top two links in George's list have been visited, whereas the Tate Gallery link has not been followed.

The standard way for the browser to demonstrate this is to have non-visited links in blue, and visited links in purple. If you look carefully, you will also notice that when you have your mouse button held down on a link it goes red. This is called the 'active link' colour. You don't have to customise these colours, but if you have a colour scheme that demands something different, just follow the instructions over the page.

Top Internet sites

- BBC News Online - We're not all going on.
- Paragon Online - Home of all my Net news!
- Tate Gallery - Who said goats can

BEGINNER: PAINTING BY NUMBERS

Step Seven An example of a **BODY** tag with link colour properties is shown below. There are three separate link colour changing properties – **LINK**, **ALINK** and **VLINK**. They don't all have to be defined together – you can just use **ALINK**, for example, and not mention the others

To make the change, first choose the colour code that you want for each of the link types. The **LINK** property defines the normal link colour, **ALINK** the 'active' link colour, and **VLINK** the 'visited' link colour.

Your completed **BODY** tag might look like this : **<BODY BGCOLOR="#FFCC00" LINK="#00FF00" ALINK="#FF0000" VLINK="#00FFFF">**. Remember to drop in your own colour codes in the right places.

```
<body bgcolor="white" link="#000099" vlink="#000099" alink="#000099">
    <table cellpadding="0" width="600" cellspacing="0" border="0">
        <tr>
            <td colspan="2"></td>
            <td colspan="3"></td>
        </tr>
        <tr>
            <td colspan="5" bgcolor="white"></td>
        </tr>
        <!-- Latest Magazines -->
        <tr>
            <td colspan="5"></td>
        </tr>
        <tr>
            <td colspan="5" bgcolor="white"></td>
        </tr>
        <tr>
            <td valign="top" bgcolor="silver">
                <table width="140" cellpadding="0" cellspa
                    <tr>
                        <td bgcolor="#000099" width=
                        <td bgcolor="#000099" width=
                    </tr>
                    <tr>
                        <td width="6" bgcolor="silver
```

BEGINNER: PAINTING BY NUMBERS

George says...

"I have chosen a tasteful shade of blue for my page background and a darker blue for my headline. It is amazing that the whole colour scheme can change so easily! Also, I have added a line to my introductory paragraph, using <I> and <B> tags to make the text italic and bold."

CHAPTER 06

BEGINNER: LISTS-U-LIKE

BEGINNER: LISTS-U-LIKE

Step One
You could quite easily create a page full of bland paragraphs, although that would not hold anybody's interest for too long. However, there are plenty of ways that HTML can step in to help and one of the easiest is to create a list.

Web browsers show lists by indenting them from the left-hand margin of the page and starting each new 'list item' with a bullet point. In fact, as the picture below shows, the tags that make lists can also be used to indent whole pages from the left margin. On the next page, you'll find out how to add a basic one to your Web page.

This excerpt from the Prospect magazine site at http://www.prospect-magazine.co.uk/ shows how lists can be employed to effectively distinguish between different sections of text

OPINIONS

NEXT TIME, SEND IN THE GURKAS
Anatol Lieven
The low tolerance of casualties among western publics mean that we may have to rely on mercenaries.

HOW MANY HOLOCAUST MUSEUMS?
Valerie Monchi
Non-religious Jews cannot depend on the Holocaust.

DOES THE CITY NEED THE EURO?
Michael Jenkins
The City of London is foreign-owned and could easily slip away.

CHINA'S YEAR OF THE ANNIVERSARY
Jonathan Spence
Tiananmen is not the only "tricky" anniversary for China's leaders this year.

DEBATE

IS GERMANY NOW THE SICK MAN OF

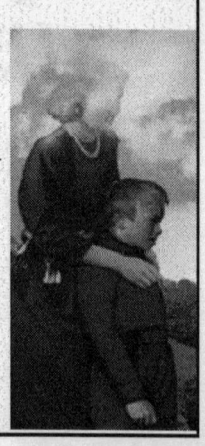

BEGINNER: LISTS-U-LIKE

Step Two You can create a simple or 'unordered' list using the **<UL>** tag, or maybe a numbered or 'ordered' list using the **<OL>** tag. Within these, each new list item is defined by the **<LI>** tag. You don't even need to use a **<P>** tag to start a new line: the **<LI>** tag does that automatically.

Remember that **<UL>** and **<OL>** must end with **</UL>** and **</OL>**, whereas **</LI>** is not required. Also, you can make 'lists within lists' by nesting extra **<UL>s** within other ones. Each extra list will be further indented from the left margin of the page.

The bulletin board section of the Internet Access Made Easy Web site at http://neteasy.paragon.co.uk/ uses <UL> lists to structure the online discussion

INTERNET @CCESS MADE EASY

The Basics   The Knack   The Net

Ask Us   The Magazine   Search

Questions & Answers

[Post Message]

- wav files on a homepage - **marie crain** *21:14:30 6/30/99* (0)
- Compuserve e-mail problem - **Chris** *17:22:48 6/27/99* (0)
- Compuserve replying - **Chris** *17:20:59 6/27/99* (0)
- E-mail with Outlook Express - **Chris** *17:18:46 6/27/99* (0)
- IE5 problem - **Chris** *17:15:46 6/27/99* (0)
- call costs - **Angel** *00:18:41 6/19/99* (0)
- disconnection - **Tegan Grigsby** *00:15:23 6/19/99* (0)
- Macs/Screaming.net - **Gareth Davies** *23:49:56 6/15/99* (0)
- Internet @ccess made easy P. 27 and P. 124 of issue 15 - **Thomas** *13:56:41 6/14/99* (1)
  - FORGET THIS THREAD - Re: Internet @ccess made easy P. 27 and P. 124 of issue 15 - **Thomas** *07:54:13 6/17/99* (0)
- cache - **don smallwood** *18:17:15 6/02/99* (0)
- teen - **girlz** *17:42:34 5/15/99* (0)
- My modem - **Pete D.** *13:00:10 3/21/99* (2)
  - Re: My modem - **Pete D** *13:07:27 3/21/99* (1)
    - Re: My modem - **Karl Foster** *17:59:26 3/25/99* (0)
- incomming calls - **Mari** *20:54:22 3/08/99* (1)
  - Re: incomming calls - **Karl Foster** *18:07:06 3/25/99* (0)
- irc and icq connections - **Ronnie Rees** *20:44:35 1/24/99* (1)
  - Re: irc and icq connections - **Geoff Harris** *09:47:10 2/03/99* (0)
- thumbnails - **Sandra Smith** *22:41:08 1/20/99* (1)
  - Re: thumbnails - **Geoff Harris** *09:51:39 2/03/99* (0)
- thumbnails - **Sandra Smith** *22:40:04 1/20/99* (0)

SceneOne www.sceneone.co.uk
- The UK's Entertainment Guide

BEGINNER: LISTS-U-LIKE

Step Three
Before plunging headlong into creating your first list, the introductory section needs to be finished off. This means making sure that the graphic you used does not interfere with the list by inserting a **<BR CLEAR=ALL>** tag at the end of the introductory paragraph.

This ensures that the next page element starts below the picture, and will not be 'aligned' alongside it like the introductory paragraph. George has added the tag in the right place on his page, as shown in the screengrab below.

```
<HR>

<IMG SRC="images/goat.gif" ALIGN="RIGHT" ALT="Self portrait of George

Hello there, my name is George the Goat and I have great pleasure in sha

My farm is in a very historic part of rural England, and I enjoy rambling

<I>Hope you enjoy the site. <B>Love from George.</B></I>
<BR CLEAR=ALL>
```

BEGINNER: LISTS-U-LIKE

Step Four Create a headline for the list. To speed things up, locate the line containing the HTML code for the main page headline (beginning **<FONT SIZE="6">**). Highlight the whole line, as shown below. To highlight, click your left mouse button at the start of the line and drag the mouse to the end, with the button still held down.

Make sure that you have highlighted all the text as far as the **</FONT><P>** tags. Now select 'Copy' from the Edit menu. Move the cursor to a fresh line after the **<BR CLEAR=ALL>** tag. Select 'Paste' from the Edit menu.

```
<TITLE>Welcome to George the Goat's Farmyard Frolics</TITLE>
</HEAD>



<BODY BGCOLOR="#ADEAEA">



<CENTER>
<FONT SIZE="6" COLOR="#236B8E">George    the   Goat's   Farmyard
Frolics!</FONT>
</CENTER>

.
<HR>
```

BEGINNER: LISTS-U-LIKE

Step Five
Change the line into a smaller size by altering **<FONT SIZE="6">** to **<FONT SIZE="4">**. Keep the same font colour – it always looks good to have a consistent colour scheme on your page.

Replace the text of the headline (ie everything between **<FONT>** and **</FONT>**) with a new headline. What you choose depends entirely on the content of the list that is to follow – for example, George chose 'My favourite things.' Of course, it isn't compulsory to give every list a headline – but in this case, it looks good and makes sure that the user understands what the list represents.

```
My farm is in a very historic part of rural England, and I enjoy
rambling around the area to take beautiful photographs of the
surroundings.<P>

<I>Hope you enjoy the site. <B>Love from George.</B></I>
<BR CLEAR=ALL>


<FONT SIZE="4" COLOR="#236B8E">My     favourite     things</FONT><BR>
```

BEGINNER: LISTS-U-LIKE

Step Six Now we are finally ready to start the list. This is the easy bit. Just make sure that your cursor is on a fresh line after the headline you have just created. Type **<UL>**, hit 'Return' a couple of times and then type **</UL>**. Everything between those tags will be considered part of the 'list' and will be indented from the left margin.

Start the list on the line after the **<UL>** tag by typing **<LI>** and entering the first list item. George has chosen to list three 'favourite things,' so he typed **<LI><B>Walking</B>** followed by a short sentence about walking. He chose to use **<B>** tags to emphasise the start of each list item – what a clever goat.

```
<FONT SIZE="4" COLOR="#236B8E">My favourite things</FONT><BR>
<UL>
<LI><B>Walking</B> - My farm is in a valley full of interesting walks and footpaths. I have
joined the goat's branch of the Ramblers Association to support the opening up of as many
rights of way as possible. I clubbed together with other animals on the farm recently and
staged a sit-in protest about our farmer blocking off rights of way.

<LI><B>Photography</B> - I was bought a camera last Christmas by the other animals, and use
it whenever I can afford the film, but mostly in the summer months. Flash photography isn't
much fun, so I use natural light all the time.

<LI><B>Going to market</B> - Sometimes we all get carted off to the market. This is
interesting, because sometimes I get moved to another farm, which adds variety to an
otherwise simple life.
</UL>
```

Build a Web Site in 24 Hours

BEGINNER: LISTS-U-LIKE

Step Seven
To add extra items to the list, add new **<LI>** tags on fresh lines. Try and format each item in the same way, so that it looks like a coherent list when displayed by the browser. For example, George's list has the keyword at the start of each line highlighted in bold.

You could follow George's example and make another list – his second list has his favourite links on it. To add a link is easy – just follow this format:
<AHREF="http://www.paragon.co.uk/">Paragon Online</A>.

Simply change the URL and linked text to suit your needs.

My favourite things

- **Walking** - My farm is in a valley full of interesting walks and footpaths. I have joined the goat's branch of the Ramblers Association to support the opening up of as many rights of way as possible. I clubbed together with other animals on the farm recently and staged a sit-in protest about our farmer blocking off rights of way.
- **Photography** - I was bought a camera last Christmas by the other animals, and use it whenever I can afford the film, but mostly in the summer months. Flash photography isn't much fun, so I use natural light all the time.
- **Going to market** - Sometimes we all get carted off to the market. This is interesting, because sometimes I get moved to another farm, which adds variety to an otherwise simple life.

BEGINNER: LISTS-U-LIKE

George says...

"I like these list things so much that I have made two of them. I was able to make the second one really quickly, by just using Copy and Paste to duplicate the first list. Then I changed the headline, and added the links."

BEGINNER: FINISHING TOUCHES

CHAPTER 07

BEGINNER: FINISHING TOUCHES

BEGINNER: FINISHING TOUCHES

Step One You've nearly finished your first Web page. But your job is not done yet. Follow these simple steps to neatly conclude your page. Position the cursor on a fresh line after your lists. Add a **<P>** tag and then a **<HR>** to draw a line across the page.

Now you need to make a note of the time and date of this 'version' of the page and you should specify who you are, together with your email address. Type 'Last updated' and then select 'Time/Date' from the Edit menu in Notepad. If you are not using Notepad, simply type the current time and date.

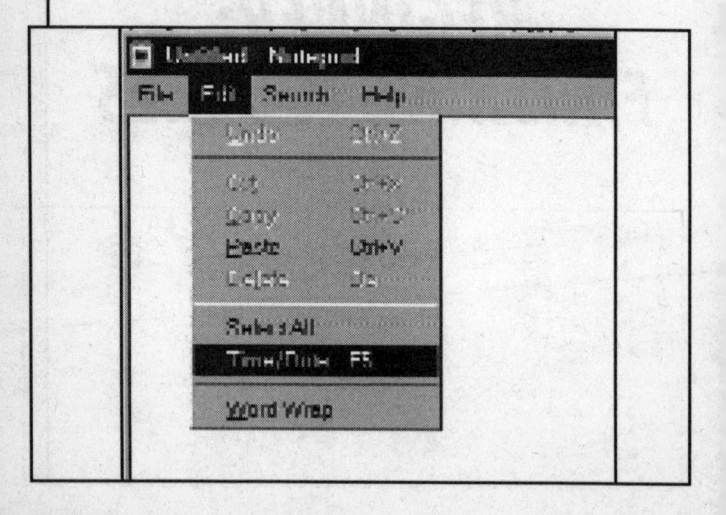

BEGINNER: FINISHING TOUCHES

Step Two Continuing with the same line as in Step One, enter your name and your email address. You can make it easy for people to email you by turning the email address into a link. For example, if you are george@goat.com, then this is done with the HTML code:

<A HREF="mailto:george@goat.com">george@goat.com</A>

Now the Web browser will highlight your email address as a hyperlink. When it is clicked on, a new email window will appear, and your address will be entered in the right place. Save the page and take a final look at it in your Web browser.

This section of the DVD Review Web site (http://www.dvdreview.net/) includes a mailto link, allowing visitors to easily get in touch with the Webmasters

BUY DIRECT

Save 10% off SRP

How to buy direct from DVD Review

1. Using our secure online ordering system. Search or browse through our database of all currently available UK DVDs using the form below.
2. Call our order hotline on (01202) 200200 (international - +44 - 1202 - 200200)
3. Fax us on (01202) 299955 (international - +44 - 1202 - 299955)
4. Email us on offers@dvdreview.net

George says...

"I'm glad to have my first Web page finished. Before I put it on the Web, I'd like to recommend some reading. Whilst I've found this guide to making a site really useful, there's a lot more to learn. Five of the best books to help take your Web site further are reviewed over the next few pages."

BEGINNER: FINISHING TOUCHES

HTML Goodies Joe Burns' excellent Web site at **http://www.htmlgoodies.com** is a great resource for Web site builders. Now Joe has written a book which crams his handy online hints and tips into four hundred pages.

To get a flavour of what you'll find in the book, take a look at his Web site – while aimed at beginners, it makes even the most advanced topics easy to understand. The dead tree version of HTML Goodies contains a real wealth of information and is well worth the cover price.

Author: Joe Burns
Price: £10.49
Publisher: Que
ISBN: 0789718235

Creative HTML Design

Lynda Weinman is one of the most authoritative and experienced Web designers to have committed their wisdom to paper. This volume is co-authored by her programmer brother and, as Lynda mentions in her bookstore at **http://www.lynda.com/bookstore**, this is a perfect match for a successful Web site – design and programming working together. This book takes the reader step-by-step through the process of making a Web site, explaining both the mechanics and the design. You can see the site for yourself at **http://www.ducks.htmlbook.com**. The only downside to the book is the hefty price tag.

Authors: Lynda & William Weinman
Price: £37.49
Publisher: New Riders
ISBN: 1562057049

BEGINNER: FINISHING TOUCHES

HTML Artistry: More Than Code

Unlike some of the titles recommended here, this book does not draw its inspiration from a popular Web site. Instead, it is based on the all-important observation that in order to make a good-looking Web site you need more than just a mastery of HTML.

Through an exploration of the additional skills required, such as effective use of graphics, visual design and user friendliness, the book explains exactly how to build a successful site. Advanced technologies and the latest browsers are discussed, which perhaps pitches this book at a higher level of understanding than the others reviewed here.

Authors: Ardith Ibanez & Natalie Zee
Price: £36.99
Publisher: New Riders
ISBN: 1568304544

Web Graphics for Dummies

The famous 'Dummies' series continues to be a runaway success with readers, mainly thanks to its consistently clear style of writing and easy-to-understand instructions. These are pretty much an essential feature of any book that attempts to tackle the complicated discipline of Web graphics.

Included with the book is a CD with various utilities and demo programs to get the reader started on graphics packages straight away. Perhaps the strangest feature of the book is that it has no colour pages, which makes demonstration of important issues such as colour tables and image quality pretty difficult.

Authors: Dummies Tech Press & Linda Richards
Price: £23.99
Publisher: IDG Books
ISBN: 0764502115

BEGINNER: FINISHING TOUCHES

Project Cool Guide to HTML

This book deliberately avoids the encyclopaedic approach taken by many other guides to HTML. This reflects the ethos of the online community from which the book takes its name (**http://www.projectcool.com**). Readers are encouraged to take a hands-on approach by testing the code and looking at the Web site created in tandem with the book.

The main complaint with this book is that it tells the reader enough to get them hooked, but then stops short of explaining the more complex technologies. Perhaps they're trying to sell the next book in the series, "ProjectCool Guide to Enhancing Your Web Site."

Authors: Teresa A. Martin & Glenn Davis
Price: £17.99
Publisher: Wiley
ISBN: 0471173711

BEGINNER: SOURCE CODE ANALYSIS

CHAPTER 08

BEGINNER: SOURCE CODE ANALYSIS

This chapter shows George's completed HTML code section by section, and compares it to the result produced in a Web browser window

Comment #1

```
<HTML>
<HEAD>
<TITLE>Welcome to George the Goat's Farmyard
Frolics</TITLE>
</HEAD>
```

These lines of code put the title into the top of the Web page. Keep this short, or it will not fit across the title bar.

BEGINNER: SOURCE CODE ANALYSIS

Comment #2

<BODY BGCOLOR="#ADEAEA">

This line is very important: it starts the main section of the page and it tells the browser to colour in the background in that tasteful shade of light blue.

Comment #3

```
<CENTER>
<FONT SIZE="6" COLOR="#236B8E">George the Goat's
Farmyard Frolics!</FONT>
</CENTER>
<HR>
```

The **<CENTER>** tag puts the headline in the middle of the page, whilst the **<FONT>** tag makes it larger than the normal font size and changes its colour to dark blue. The line underneath is thanks to the **<HR>** tag.

BEGINNER: SOURCE CODE ANALYSIS

Comment #4

`<IMG SRC="images/goat.gif" ALIGN="RIGHT" ALT="Self portrait of George">`

This line tells the Web browser to look in the directory called 'images' for a file named 'goat.gif.' Then it must align the picture to the right of the text that follows. George has included an **ALT** tag, which appears whilst the image is loading – but it isn't very important.

George the Goat's Farmyard Frolics!

Hello there, my name is George the Goat and I have great pleasure in sharing with you my Farmyard Frolics. Contrary to the fantastical tales you may have read about farms, there is actually very little that goes on. To avoid complete boredom, I picked up a copy of Practical Internet from the local newsagent and created this page.

My farm is in a very historic part of rural England, and I enjoy rambling around the area to take beautiful photographs of the surroundings.

Hope you enjoy the site. ***Love from George.***

My favourite things

- **Walking** - My farm is in a valley full of interesting walks and footpaths. I have joined the goat's branch of the Ramblers Association to support the opening up of as many rights of way as possible. I clubbed together with other animals on the farm recently and staged a sit-in protest about our farmer blocking off rights of way.
- **Photography** - I was bought a camera last Christmas by the other animals, and use it whenever I can afford the film, but mostly in the summer months. Flash photography isn't much fun, so I use natural light all the time.
- **Going to market** - Sometimes we all get carted off to the market. This is interesting, because sometimes I get moved to another farm, which adds variety to an otherwise simple life.

Top Internet sites

- BBC News Online - We're not allowed to watch TV on the farm, so this site keeps me up to date with what's going on.
- Paragon Online - Home of all my favourite magazines - I always visit Paragon Online for top video game and Net news!
- Tate Gallery - Who said goats can't appreciate art? Top site!

Last updated 15:19 27/06/98 - Created using Notepad by George the Goat.

BEGINNER: SOURCE CODE ANALYSIS

Comment #5

Hello there, my name is George the Goat and I have great pleasure in sharing with you my Farmyard Frolics. Contrary to the fantastical tales you may have read about farms, there is actually very little that goes on. To avoid complete boredom, I picked up a copy of Practical Internet from the local newsagent and created this page.<P>

My farm is in a very historic part of rural England, and I enjoy rambling around the area to take beautiful photographs of the surroundings.<P>
<I>Hope you enjoy the site. <B>Love from George.</B></I>
<BR CLEAR=ALL>

These are George's opening comments, divided into paragraphs with the **<P>** tag. You can also use a **
** tag to just start a new line, without adding a blank line in the middle. Note also that George used italics and bold text on the last line. The final part of code draws an 'invisible line' beneath this part of the page.

George the Goat's Farmyard

Hello there, my name is George the Goat and I have great pleasure in sharing with you my Farmyard Frolics. Contrary to the fantastical tales you may have read about farms, there is actually very little that goes on. To avoid complete boredom, I picked up a copy of Practical Internet from the local newsagent and created this page.

My farm is in a very historic part of rural England, and I enjoy rambling around the area to take beautiful photographs of the surroundings.

Hope you enjoy the site. ***Love from George.***

BEGINNER: SOURCE CODE ANALYSIS

Comment #6

```
<FONT SIZE="4" COLOR="#236B8E">My favourite
things</FONT><BR>
<UL>
<LI><B>Walking</B> – My farm is in a valley full of
interesting walks and footpaths. I have joined the goat's
branch of the Ramblers Association to support the
opening up of as many rights of way as possible. I
clubbed together with other animals on the farm
recently and staged a sit-in protest about our farmer
blocking off rights of way.
<LI><B>Photography</B> – I was bought a camera last
Christmas by the other animals, and use it whenever I
can afford the film, but mostly in the summer months.
Flash photography isn't much fun, so I use natural light
all the time.
<LI><B>Going to market</B> – Sometimes we all get
carted off to the market. This is interesting, because
sometimes I get moved to another farm, which adds
variety to an otherwise simple life.
</UL>
```

This entire section is the first of George's lists. First of all, he uses a headline, and then three **<LI>** tags within the **<UL>** structure to make three distinct list items.

My favourite things

- **Walking** - My farm is in a valley full of interesting walks and footpaths. I have joined the goat's branch of the Ramblers Association to support the opening up of as many rights of way as possible. I clubbed together with other animals on the farm recently and staged a sit-in protest about our farmer blocking off rights of way.
- **Photography** - I was bought a camera last Christmas by the other animals, and use it whenever I can afford the film, but mostly in the summer months. Flash photography isn't much fun, so I use natural light all the time.
- **Going to market** - Sometimes we all get carted off to the market. This is interesting, because sometimes I get moved to another farm, which adds variety to an otherwise simple life.

Build a Web Site in 24 Hours

Comment #7

```
<FONT SIZE="4" COLOR="#236B8E">Top Internet
sites</FONT><BR>
<UL>
<LI><A HREF="http://news.bbc.co.uk/">BBC News
Online</A> - We're not allowed to watch TV on the
farm, so this site keeps me up to date with what's going
on.
<LI><A HREF="http://www.paragon.co. uk/">Paragon
Online</A> - Home of all my favourite magazines - I
always visit Paragon Online for top video game and Net
news!
<LI><A HREF="http://www.tate.org.uk/">Tate
Gallery</A> - Who said goats can't appreciate art? Top
site!
</UL>
```

This second list is a duplicate of the first, with altered details. As George explained earlier, you can easily make a link to another Web site just by using the **<A HREF>** tag.

Top Internet sites

- BBC News Online - We're not allo
- Paragon Online - Home of all my fa
- Tate Gallery - Who said goats can't

BEGINNER: SOURCE CODE ANALYSIS

Comment #8

```
<P>
<HR>
<SMALL>Last updated 15:19 27/06/98 – Created using
Notepad by George the Goat.</SMALL>
</BODY>
</HTML>
```

These final lines of code are the polite way to the end the page. They tell any visitors when the page was last updated and who did the update. Note that George has put this information in a smaller size of font by using the **<SMALL>** tag. The final two tags of the code close off the page to the browser's satisfaction.

- BBC News Online - We're not all
- Paragon Online - Home of all my f
- Tate Gallery - Who said goats can'

Last updated 15:19 27/06/98 - Created using No

CHAPTER 09

BEGINNER: GETTING IT ONLINE

BEGINNER: GETTING IT ONLINE

Step One Now that the page itself is completed, you need to put it online for the world to see. Of course, in order to do this you will need to have some Web space – perhaps from your ISP, or alternatively from one of the 'free space' providers on the Net. If you don't have anywhere to host your site at the moment, five of the better free space providers are listed on the next few pages.

The most common route of getting your site online is via FTP (File Transfer Protocol), which is a way for you to send your Web page to another computer called a 'server' using a special piece of software. This sounds complicated, but it is a simple process. The diagram below shows how your computer, the server and the Web are linked together.

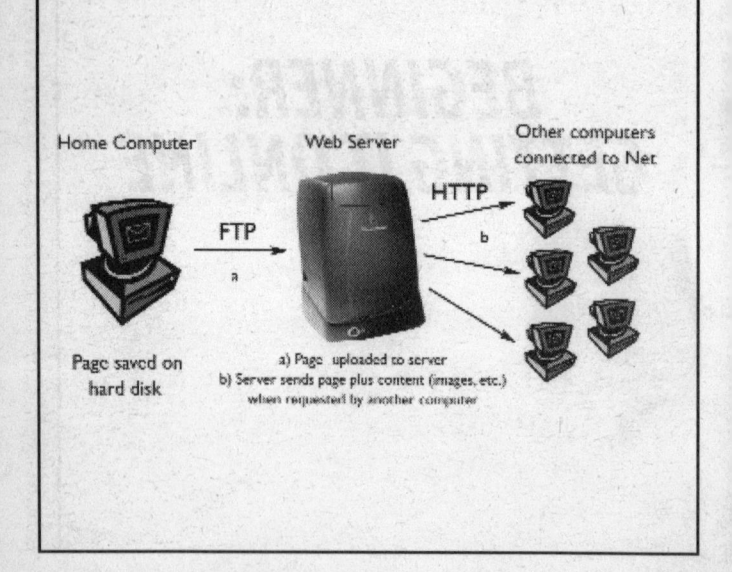

Home Computer — FTP → Web Server — HTTP → Other computers connected to Net

Page saved on hard disk

a) Page uploaded to server
b) Server sends page plus content (images, etc.) when requested by another computer

BEGINNER: GETTING IT ONLINE

089

Fortune City

http://www.fortunecity.com/

Much more than just a free Web space provider, FortuneCity is an entire online community that is well worth joining. You get free email and the ability to participate in online chat and events by signing up.

GeoCities

http://www.geocities.com/
The original free Web page provider continues to be one of the most popular, even after its recent takeover by Net directory Yahoo! But you do have to put up with either pop-up adverts or a GeoCities panel on each page.

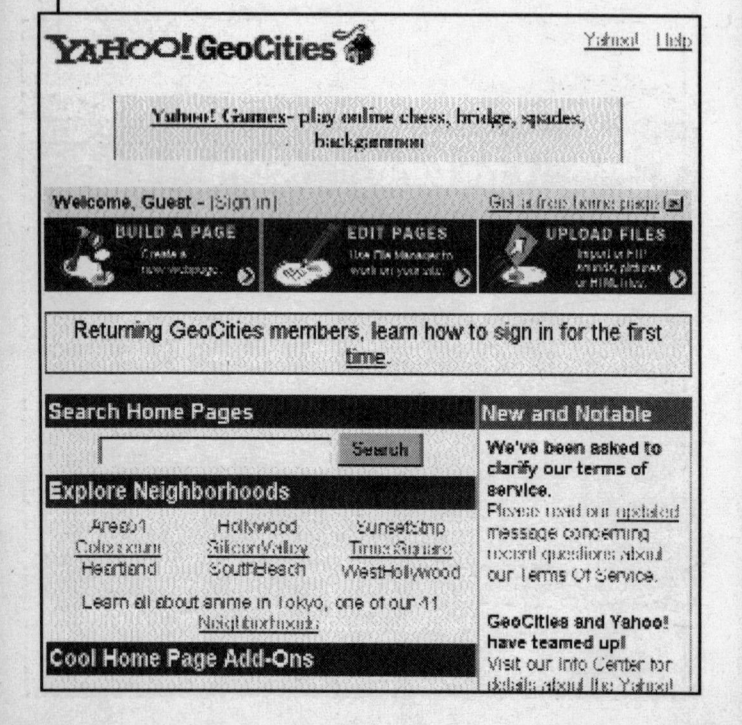

BEGINNER: GETTING IT ONLINE

Tripod UK

http://www.tripod.co.uk/

This is a fabulous Web site that has a great community feel, plus plenty of help for the novice Web site author. Many add-ons are freely available for Web pages hosted here, such as visitor counters.

Xoom

http://www.xoom.com/

Xoom claims to offer free Web sites with no restrictions on the amount of hard disk space they occupy. Fast, reliable servers and free bonuses such as clipart and chat rooms make this a popular choice.

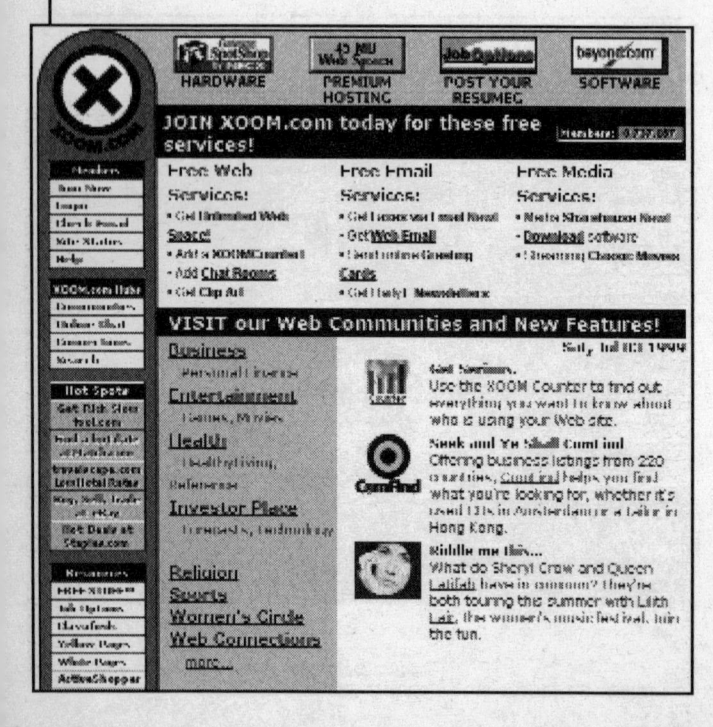

BEGINNER: GETTING IT ONLINE

Spree

http://www.spree.com/

The aim of Spree is more along the lines of providing free online shops than Web sites, but you're ultimately free to use the space as you wish. There are plenty of affiliate systems available through Spree which might help you make some cash out of your Web site.

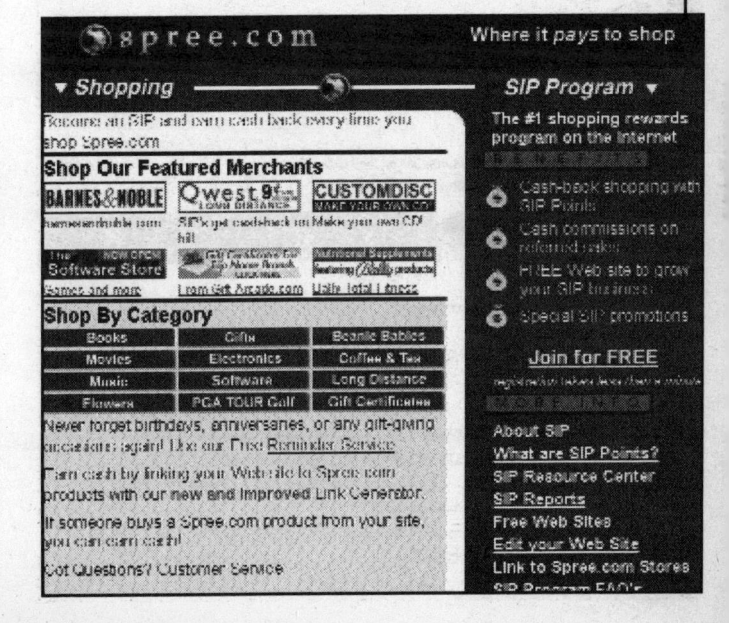

Before uploading

The first step before you upload your page is to make sure that you know what your ISP's arrangements are – these will probably be published on their Web site, or available by contacting their help desk.

All you are doing by transferring files over FTP is copying them onto another hard drive. In order to make sure that they reach the right place on the right hard drive, you'll need to know certain information before you start. This is shown across the page.

Most ISPs provide your connection information on their Web site, as shown here with Freeserve (http://www.freeserve.net/)

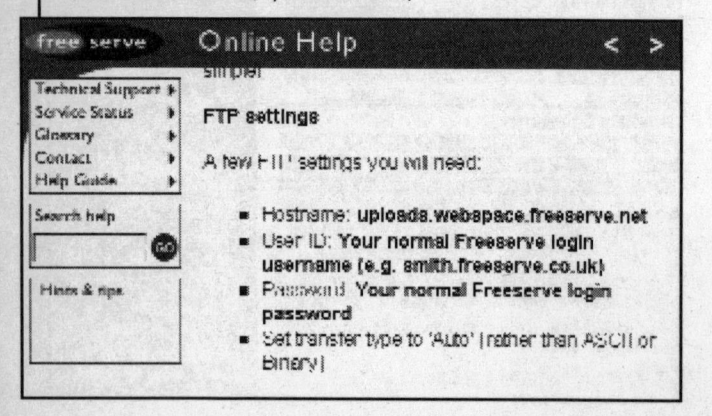

FTP settings

A few FTP settings you will need:

- Hostname: **uploads.webspace.freeserve.net**
- User ID: **Your normal Freeserve login username (e.g. smith.freeserve.co.uk)**
- Password: **Your normal Freeserve login password**
- Set transfer type to 'Auto' (rather than ASCII or Binary)

BEGINNER: GETTING IT ONLINE

Essential information

- **Information** — **Typical example**
  Notes

- **Username** — **johnsmith**
  This is case sensitive, so be sure to get it right!

- **Password** — **(A secret word)**
  If you're using ISP Web space, this will probably be the same as your dialup password.

- **FTP server address** — **ftp.geocities.com**
  Normally (but not always) begins with 'ftp'.

- **Directory for uploading** — **public_html**
  You might not need to know this, as some servers automatically present you with the correct directory.

- **Index file name** — **index.html**
  An address like http://www.paragon.co.uk/george/ will actually display the HTML index file for that directory, which is normally called index.html. Check with your Web space provider to see if they use a different index file name, and make sure that your main page has that name.

CHAPTER 10

BEGINNER: ON THE UPLOAD

BEGINNER: ON THE UPLOAD

Step One To use FTP, you'll need some client software. We'll be using WSFTP, which is available as a free download (LE version) from **http://www.ipswitch.com/**. There are various other FTP packages available, all of which would be equally suitable to the task in hand. We're using WSFTP here as it is a small download and incredibly simple to use. Macintosh users should look out for Fetch, which is the best shareware solution for their platform.

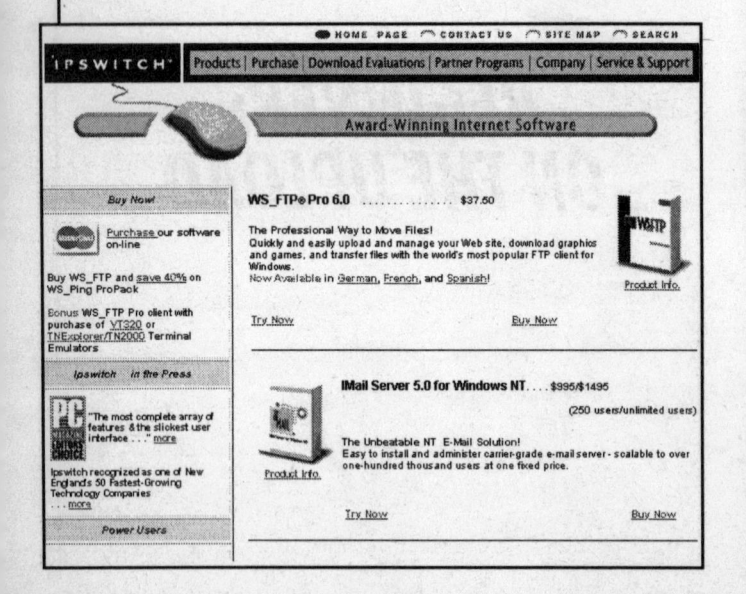

BEGINNER: ON THE UPLOAD

099

Step Two This screen appears when WSFTP is launched for the first time. It allows you to store your connection information so you'll never have to type it in again. Click 'New' to begin. Type a name for this configuration into the Profile Name box. Put the FTP server address into the Host Name box, then put your User ID and Password in their respective boxes. Check the 'Save Password' box, and click 'OK' to connect.

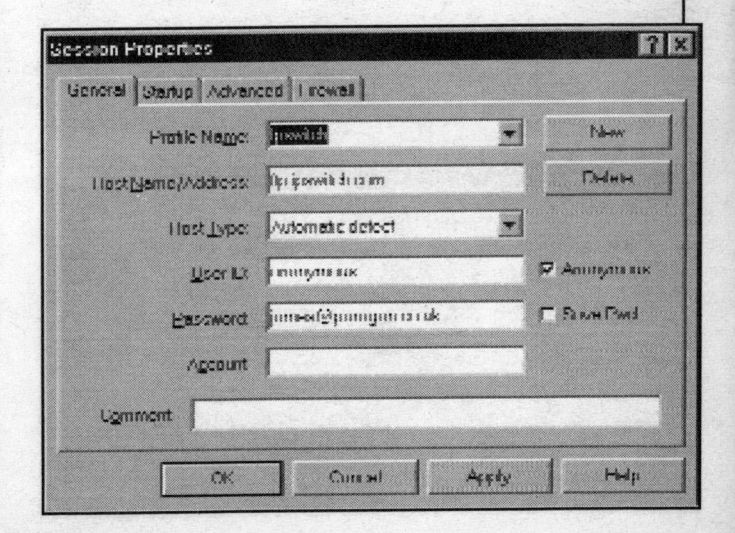

Build a Web Site in 24 Hours — Chapter 10

BEGINNER: ON THE UPLOAD

Step Three Once the connection is established, there will be two hard drive file listings: your local machine on the left, and the FTP server on the right. By clicking your way through the directories of your hard disk, bring up the folder containing your Web site. Select all of the files in your hard disk's Web site directory, by single-clicking on the first in the list, and holding down shift whilst you single-click on the last in the list.

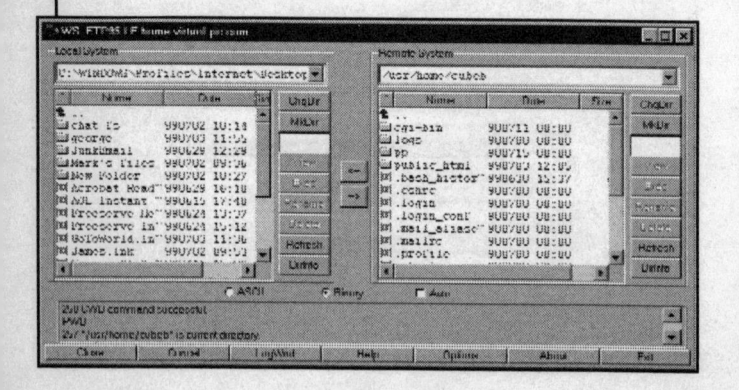

BEGINNER: ON THE UPLOAD

Step Four Make sure that the right-hand side of the screen is showing the correct directory for file uploading. Then click the right-arrow button, which is located between the two file listings. If the dialogue box pictured above appears, click 'Yes.' Don't worry if the file listings change whilst the transfer is in progress – this is normal. As each file transfers, you will see a progress bar indicating how much data has been sent.

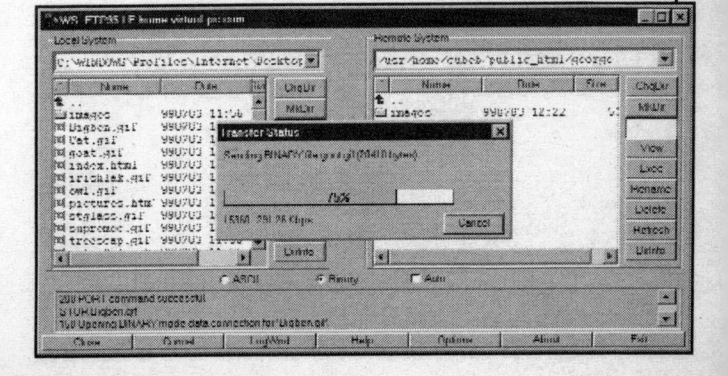

BEGINNER: ON THE UPLOAD

Step Five
When the transfers stop, check through both of the file listings to ensure that all the files have been uploaded. If individual files need to be resent, simply single-click their names on the hard drive listing and click the right arrow button again. But make sure each time that both the left and right-hand panels of the screen are logged into the same directory, or you will end up sending the files into the wrong place on the FTP server.

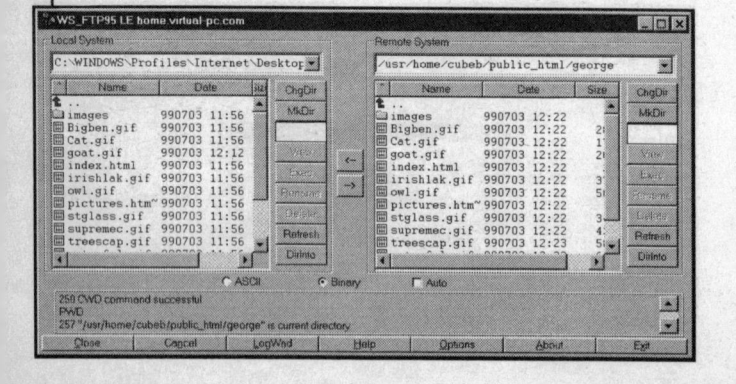

BEGINNER: ON THE UPLOAD

Step Six Quit out of WSFTP. Launch your Web browser, and type in your Web page address. Your page should then appear – check through any links and ensure that all the images are in place. If you change your Web page in any way – such as altering graphics, as below, or maybe updating the HTML itself – you needn't resend the entire site. Just follow the instructions on the next page.

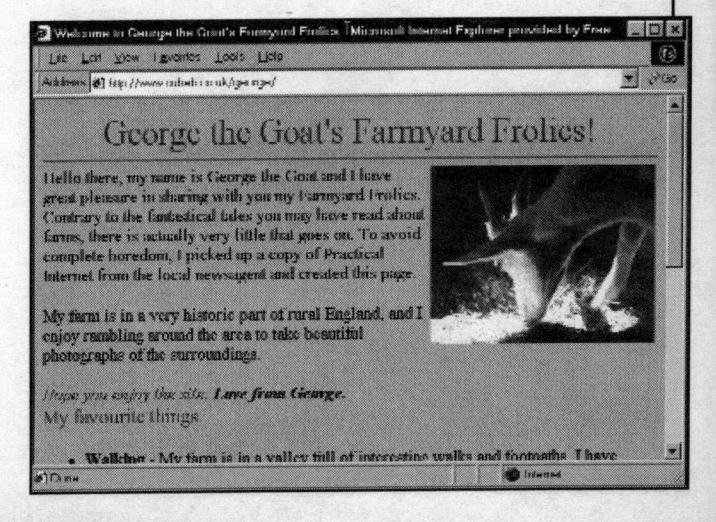

BEGINNER: ON THE UPLOAD

Step Seven

Firstly, connect to the FTP server. Click the 'Date' tab at the top of both the left and right-hand listings. This places the most recently changed files at the top of the list. Select the changed files, and transfer them by clicking the right-arrow button again. Review the page in your Web browser each time you upload a file by FTP, to ensure that the file transferred properly and is in place. You may have to press the 'Refresh' or 'Reload' button to get the new page or graphic to display.

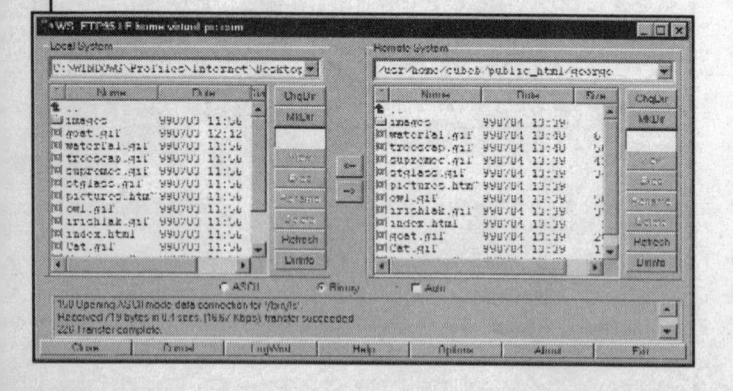

BEGINNER: ON THE UPLOAD

George says "At last I am online. It took some doing, but eventually I figured out how to use WS_FTP properly. I am very proud to be the first goat to launch himself into cyberspace. Thank you Practical Internet."

George has joined Angelfire, at **http://www.angelfire.com**, which provides free Web space and an easy 'Web Shell' to upload your pages to the Net without using FTP. It doesn't get much easier than that!

CHAPTER 11

INTERMEDIATE: TEXTUAL INTERCOURSE

Find out how to jazz up your text with lists, lines, fonts and tables

INTERMEDIATE: TEXTUAL INTERCOURSE

Lists

Lists are one of the easiest ways to bring order where chaos would otherwise reign. In the world of HTML, there are two basic kinds of list – unordered and ordered. Unordered lists are based around bullet points, while ordered lists are numbered. An unordered list is defined by the tag **<UL>**, which must encloses all of the list items – defined by the tag **<LI>**. Rather confusingly, **</LI>** is not required.

- <u>This is a list of links</u>
- <u>which is one way of using the UL tag</u>
- <u>to good effect, because it attracts</u>
- <u>the user's attention.</u>

1. This sort of list lets you index things by number
2. Perhaps your favourite movies of all time?
3. Maybe your top ten Web sites?

INTERMEDIATE: TEXTUAL INTERCOURSE

Bullet points

The type of bullet point that's used for a list can also be specified by adding a property to the main tag – **<UL TYPE = "SQUARE">** would give hollow square bullets. The other two types are **CIRCLE** (hollow circles) and **DISC** (solid circles – the default). So, the example shown below uses **<UL>** and **<LI>** tags, with **<A HREF>** tags thrown in to create the links. These different styles of bullet points don't appear in all of the browsers, as they're no longer part of the official HTML standard.

Ordered lists are also easy to make and are a useful way of creating tidy lists without having to remember what list item number you are working on.

- This list has uses SQUARE type bullets
- This list has uses DISC type bullets
- This list has uses CIRCLE type bullets

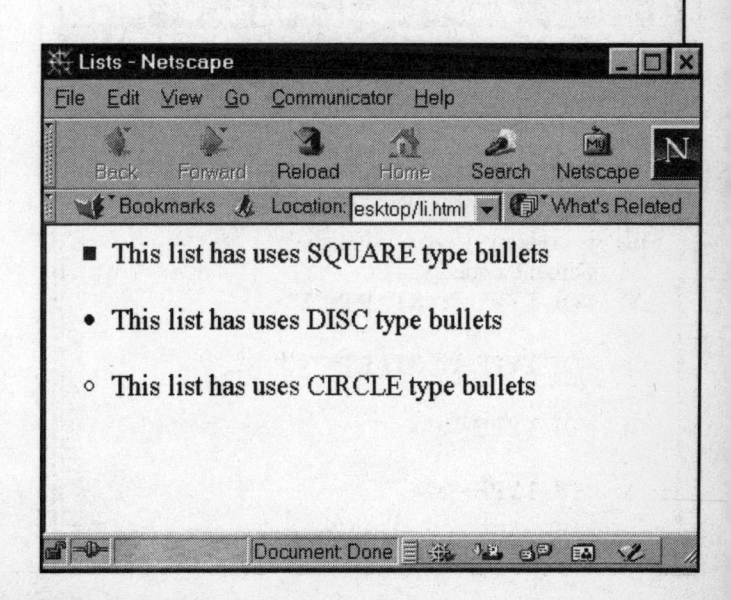

Numbered lists

In fact, ordered lists can have roman numerals, letters or numbers as the indexing unit, and the user can specify what list number to start with. Again, the **<OL>** tag must surround all **<LI>** tags. To specify a different indexing unit or start point, the tag changes to **<OL TYPE = "i" START = "3">**. That example would use lower-case roman numerals, starting with 'iii.' The other **TYPE** options you can have are I (upper-case roman numerals), a (lower-case letters), A (upper-case letters), and 1 (numbers – the default).

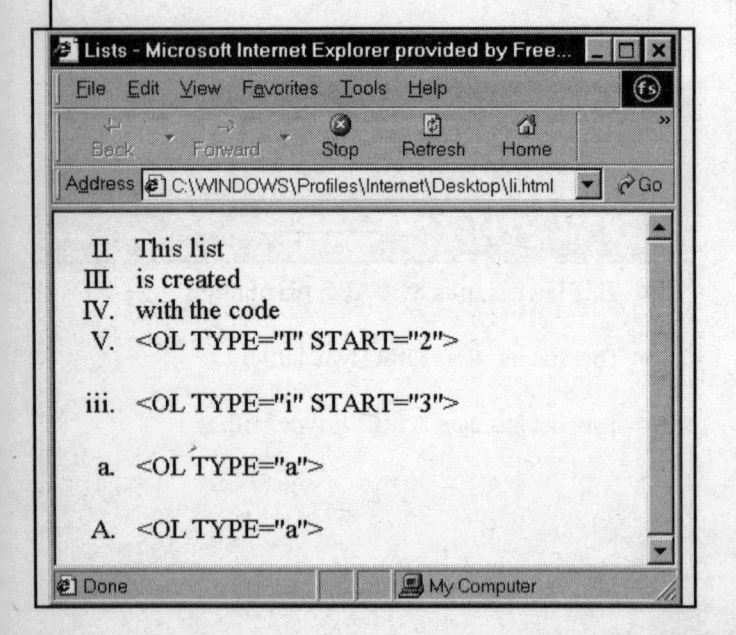

Lists - Microsoft Internet Explorer provided by Free...

Address: C:\WINDOWS\Profiles\Internet\Desktop\li.html

II. This list
III. is created
IV. with the code
V. <OL TYPE="I" START="2">

iii. <OL TYPE="i" START="3">

a. <OL TYPE="a">

A. <OL TYPE="a">

INTERMEDIATE: TEXTUAL INTERCOURSE

Horizontal rules
Moving on from lists, the horizontal rule tag **<HR>** is used mercilessly on many thousands of Web sites. However, very few people bother using its full potential – namely, to change the size, width, colour, alignment and opacity of the rule. Widths can be specified in percentages of the window, or pixels; size can only be specified in pixels, while colours can be named or the hex code quoted. The example shown is a 200 by 3 pixel line, coloured red and aligned to the left. The actual HTML code used is **<HR WIDTH = "30%" ALIGN = LEFT SIZE = "2" COLOR = "RED">**.

HRs accompany headlines well

More on lists and rules

As demonstrated on the previous page, the **<HR>** tag can be a stylish way of underlining headlines. However, Netscape Navigator doesn't represent the colour of the line – only Internet Explorer currently supports this feature.

The opacity of the line defaults to embossed see-through, but can be changed by adding the word 'SOLID' to the tag. Internet Explorer renders coloured rules solid by default. If you want more info about using rules and lists, take a look a Jeff Walters' site, 'HTML Tutorials for the Complete Idiot' at **http://www.geocities.com/SiliconValley/Campus/1924**.

HTML Tutorials
for the
Complete Idiot
By Jeff Walters

HTML help! Webpage help! Homepage help! These HTML tutorials have been designed to help people build better home pages the easy way. Step by step tutorials in plain English will enable you to gain the knowledge needed; HTML tips, tricks, and techniques. Web page design tools, lists, tables, META tags, backgrounds, images, page jumps, fonts, headings, color codes, guestbooks, chat rooms, and many other instructional resources.

INTERMEDIATE: TEXTUAL INTERCOURSE

Font fiddling

There's plenty of design tweaking potential with fonts, as well. Using the **FACE** property of the **<FONT>** tag, it's possible to change the text styling on your Web pages.

While it's not a very good idea to specify any old font in this way, there are certain typefaces that are available on the vast majority of computers. As well as the standard Times and Courier, the basic range of Microsoft fonts are automatically installed alongside Internet Explorer and on most Windows systems.

Brush up on all the latest developments in Web fonts at http://www.webfonts.com/

The next innovation in Web design will allow designers to use fonts and control the size, color, placement and kerning of type on the Web. Enter the era of Embedded and Dynamic Fonts.

Microsoft fonts

Microsoft's suite of Web fonts include Arial, Verdana, Trebuchet MS and Georgia. The first three are sans serif faces, all of which are fairly similar. Georgia is a Times lookalike that was specifically designed for use on a screen rather than in print. To use these fonts, simply use tags like **<FONT FACE = "Georgia, serif" SIZE = "5">** where required. The reason for the word 'serif' being used is to let Web browsers without Georgia display a similar font. For sans serif fonts, simply put 'sans-serif' in its place. If you want to apply the font across the whole document, you need to use stylesheets, which are explained in Chapter 13 of this book.

Why not try some different font faces, such as the standard Microsoft fonts: Arial is easy to read, Verdana was designed especially for the computer screen, Trebuchet is yet another sans-serif offering, but smart Georgia is an attractive alternative to Times.

INTERMEDIATE: TEXTUAL INTERCOURSE

Simple tables

Although tables are more fully covered in Chapter 16 of this book, in their most simple form they can be useful for highlighting sections of text. In fact, they can have the greatest visual impact when used simply as single cell panels with a background and possibly a border. Simply use the HTML shown below, and alter the size, border, colour and alignment options to suit your needs.

```
<TABLE WIDTH = "50%" HEIGHT = "100" BORDER = "2"
BGCOLOR = "yellow"> <TR VALIGN = CENTER ALIGN =
CENTER> <TD><FONT SIZE = 4 FACE = "Georgia, serif"
COLOR = "blue">
  Simple tables make excellent text holding devices. The
example shown highlights the content away from the rest of
the page and gives a very impressive finish.
</FONT> </TD></TR></TABLE>
```

> Simple tables make excellent text holding devices. This example highlights the content away from the rest of the page with quite impressive visual effect.

CHAPTER 12

INTERMEDIATE: ENDLESS ENTITIES

If you want to place special characters on your Web pages, you need to use the codes shown in this chapter instead of typing the character directly into the HTML code. Simply add the code where the letter is required and it will be translated into the relevant character by the Web browser

Hyphenation & punctuation

" = "
& = &
¡ = ¡
¨ = ¨
´ = ´
« = «
» = »

If you're putting together Web pages in French, these entity codes will come in very useful, as seen in use here at http://www.lemonde.fr/

INTERMEDIATE: ENDLESS ENTITIES

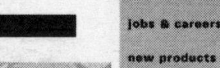

Maths symbols

< = <
> = >
¬ = ≠
± = ±
µ = µ
÷ = ÷
° = °
º = º
§ = §
ª = ª

If you divide your time between reading Nature at http://www.nature.com/ and putting your scientific experiments online, these entities will be invaluable

Acute accents

Á = Á
É = É
Í = Í
Ó = Ó
Ú = Ú
á = á
é = é
í = í
ó = ó
ú = ú

It's also possible to use text versions of these entity codes, instead of the numbers as shown here. Take a look at http://www.cl.cam.ac.uk/~and1000/entities.html to find out more

ISO Latin1 Character Entity Reference

[[This web page was shamelessly lifted from http://numinous.com/_private/people/pjl/latin1_reference.html]]

Here are the ISO Latin1 character entities as lifted from the I18N Internationalization Internet Draft. The first column contains the actual characters to be displayed, the second column contains the text to include within your HTML document to get the corresponding characters to display, and the third column contains the character descriptions listed in the internationalization draft. And yes, despite the fact that the em dash is the most useful non-alphanumeric character on the planet, it's not in the list:

      no-break space

INTERMEDIATE: ENDLESS ENTITIES

Grave accents

À = À
È = È
Ì = Ì
Ò = Ò
Ù = Ù
à = à
è = è
ì = ì
ò = ò
ù = ù

This Irish Web site at http://cce.irish-music.net/ successfully uses accented characters in its title bar, with entities in the <TITLE> tag

---

Irish Music Festivals Listing 1999 **and** discussions (new)

CCE - latest Treoir

The Official

*C*omhaltas *C*eoltóirí *E*ireann

Web Site

Fáilte(Welcome) to the Comhaltas Ceoltóirí Eireann Web Site.

Comhaltas Ceoltóirí Eireann was formed in Mullingar in 1951. At that time Irish traditional music and other traditions were in danger of being ignored. In the intervening years, thousands of people who supported

Circumflexes

Â = Â
Ê = Ê
Î = Î
Ô = Ô
Û = Û
â = â
ê = ê
î = î
ô = ô
û = û

If you're seriously into foreign languages, pay a visit to the Accent on Type site at http://www.aot.co.uk/ for all the IT solutions you'll ever need...

Accent on type
THE ONE STOP WORLD LANGUAGE SHOP

LANGUAGE
- ENGLISH
- ARABIC
- FRENCH
- GERMAN
- JAPANESE
- RUSSIAN
- SPANISH

Bienvenue

Please choose your language now.

INTERMEDIATE: ENDLESS ENTITIES

Umlauts

Ä = Ä
Ë = Ë
Ï = Ï
Ö = Ö
Ü = Ü
ä = ä
ë = ë
ï = ï
ö = ö
ü = ü

German magazine site Spiegel (http://www.spiegel.de/) just wouldn't be the same without a smattering of umlaut entities

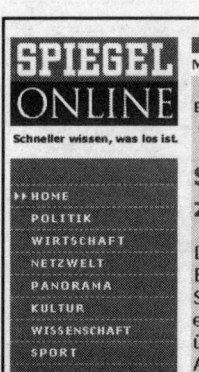

Other accented letters

Ã = Ã
Ñ = Ñ
Õ = Õ
ã = ã
ñ = ñ
õ = õ
Ø = Ø
ç = ç
Å = Å
å = å
Ç = Ç
ø = ø

*Put the 'ñ' in Yahoo España (http://www.yahoo.es/)
with the help of these entity codes*

INTERMEDIATE: ENDLESS ENTITIES

Miscellanea

  = (Non-breaking space)
· = · (Small bullet point)
¿ = ¿
æ = æ
ß = ß
Æ = Æ
¶ = ¶
¢ = ¢
£ = £
¥ = ¥
© = ©
® = ®

If you need currency symbols on your site, use these entities,
and pay a visit to the free conversion service at
http://www.xe.net/ucc/

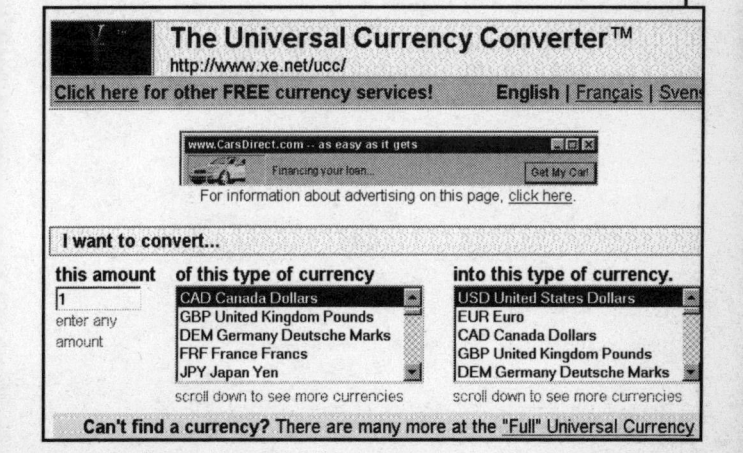

The Universal Currency Converter™
http://www.xe.net/ucc/

Click here for other FREE currency services!   English | Français | Sven

www.CarsDirect.com -- as easy as it gets
Financing your loan...   Get My Car!

For information about advertising on this page, click here.

I want to convert...

this amount	of this type of currency	into this type of currency.
1	CAD Canada Dollars	USD United States Dollars
enter any amount	GBP United Kingdom Pounds	EUR Euro
	DEM Germany Deutsche Marks	CAD Canada Dollars
	FRF France Francs	GBP United Kingdom Pounds
	JPY Japan Yen	DEM Germany Deutsche Marks
	scroll down to see more currencies	scroll down to see more currencies

Can't find a currency? There are many more at the "Full" Universal Currency

CHAPTER 13

INTERMEDIATE: STYLESHEETS MADE SIMPLE

INTERMEDIATE: STYLESHEETS MADE SIMPLE

When creating a Web site, one of the most difficult feats is ensuring consistency across the design. For example, if you want to have all your headlines in the font Verdana at size **<H2>** and coloured blue, then you have to keep on typing (or cutting and pasting) the same formatting code over and over again.

More frustrating still is when you have entered **<H2><FONT FACE="Verdana" COLOR="blue">** 17 times over and you then realise that you meant to use Georgia as the font. It is obvious that these complicated efforts are simply too much for some Web designers, which explains why so many sites lack any kind of consistent design.

The entire look of the DVD Review Web site at http://www.dvdreview.net/ can be changed by altering a single stylesheet file. This sort of design flexibility is essential with sites of all sizes

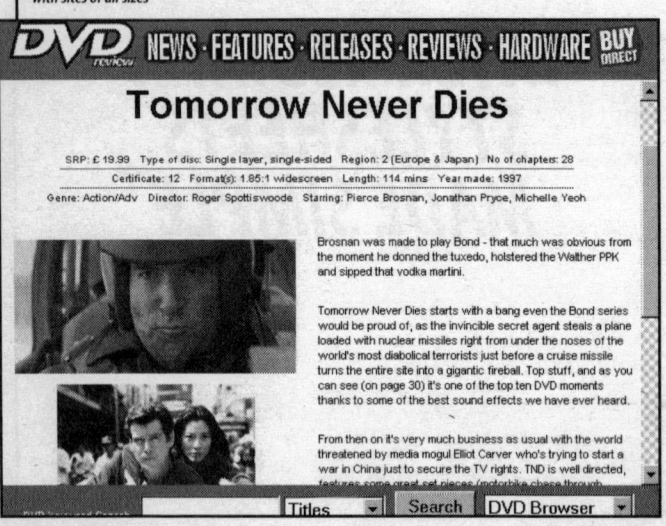

INTERMEDIATE: STYLESHEETS MADE SIMPLE

The sweat and toil of having to update **<FONT>** tags across an entire site can be avoided thanks to the widespread recognition of Cascading Style Sheets (CSS) by most Web browsers. Users of word processors or desktop publishing software will be familiar with the idea of styles – simply define the format once, and then it is available for repeated use throughout a document.

Later, if you change your mind about the style, you can easily alter the master setting and all of the relevant changes will happen automatically. It is very simple to get this sort of system up and running on your home page – and as you will soon find out, it pushes the boundaries of Web design even further by enabling you to control the appearance of your pages more than ever before.

The World Wide Web Consortium (http://www.w3.org/) is in charge of shaping official Net standards, including the CSS standard for stylesheets

W3C WORLD WIDE WEB
consortium

Leading the Web to its Full Potential...

W3C Issues Recommendation for Associating Style Sheets with XML Documents

The latest W3C Recommendation, "Associating Style Sheets with XML documents", provides authors with an interoperable mechanism for adding style to XML documents. *"Style sheets are an essential step in XML deployment, as without them there is no way to define the presentation of XML*

User Interface Domain
- HTML
- Style Sheets: CSS, XSL
- Document Object Model: DOM
- Synchronized Multimedia: SMIL
- Math: MathML
- Graphics: SVG, WebCGM
- Voice Browser
- Internationalization
- Mobile Access

Technology and Society Domain
- Electronic Commerce
- Metadata: RDF, PICS
- Privacy: P3P
- XML Signature

Architecture Domain
- HTTP, HTTP-NG
- Television and the Web

INTERMEDIATE: STYLESHEETS MADE SIMPLE

Let's start with the example given on the previous page, and convert the formatting information for our headline into a style. The simplest way to include styles in your Web pages is to make them part of the **<HEAD>** section – probably the only other thing there at the moment will be your **<TITLE>** and possibly the odd **<SCRIPT>**. Anyway, this is the code that we need to add:

```
<STYLE TYPE="text/css">
<!--
h2      { font-family: Verdana; color: blue }
-->
</STYLE>
```

If you're interested in learning more about CSS,
take a look at the tutorial series at
http://www.htmlgoodies.com/beyond/css.html

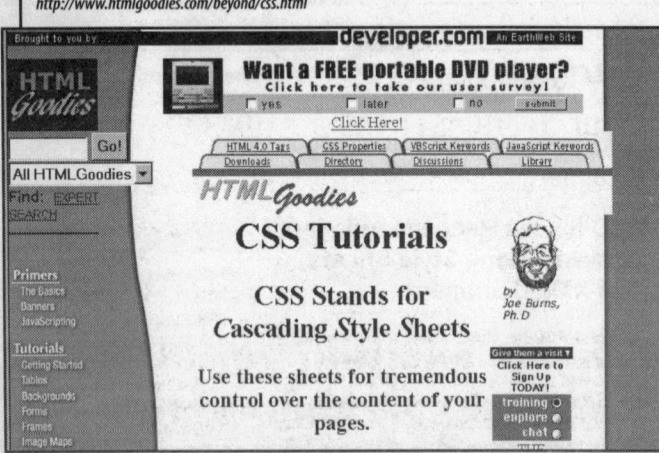

INTERMEDIATE: STYLESHEETS MADE SIMPLE

Looking back at the code on the last page, the first and last two lines are simply standard padding. These let the browser know there is a style definition coming, and then hide it from older browsers to prevent them displaying it as part of the Web page.

The all-important line is the one that starts 'h2' as it redefines what the browser will display whenever it comes across an **<H2>** tag in the HTML code. Note that the 'h2' is separated from the curly brackets by a single tab, and that the convention is to define styles in lower case, separated by semi-colons. In this example, the browser will render the text in blue Verdana instead of the default (probably black Times).

This shows the effect on the appearance of H2 text using the example style code provided

before

Your average H2 text - black Times.

after

A more exciting variation, thanks to stylesheets

INTERMEDIATE: STYLESHEETS MADE SIMPLE

Our example works fine, although it does use a fair amount of brute force. What happens if you want to use **<H2>** size text that isn't a headline and thus shouldn't really appear in blue Verdana? This is why there are different ways of defining and applying styles, which allow you to create your own formats rather than redefine existing ones.

The method of definition is pretty similar, but the way you use it is different. As an example, let's say that our Web page contains lots of quotations from Shakespeare, which need to appear in a distinct format to the rest of the text. In fact, each quotation will be given its own paragraph so that it positively shines off the page.

The full list of CSS properties can be found at http://www.projectcool.com/developer/reference/css_style.html, with a handy guide to which currently work with Navigator and Explorer

developerzone

get a FREE gift from PC World Gear

CSS Style Properties

This section summarizes the five style properties of supported by Cascading Style Sheets. Sc through the file or click on one of the style properties below.

The symbol **N** means that the style property is not supported by Netscape Navigator 4.0.

The symbol means that the style property is not supported by Internet Explorer 3.0.

The symbol **4.0** means that the style property is not supported by Internet Explorer 4.0.

INTERMEDIATE: STYLESHEETS MADE SIMPLE

We want to use the Arial font, coloured dark green, in 14 point type, aligned to the centre of the page, with an indent from the left-hand margin to separate the quote from the rest of the text. To demonstrate how stylesheets go beyond the normal limits of HTML text formatting, we'll also throw in a light yellow background for good measure. This style is defined by adding the following code to the **<HEAD>** section of a Web page:

```
<STYLE TYPE="text/css">
<!--
.quotation { font-family: Arial; background: lightyellow;
color: darkgreen; font-size: 14px;
text-align: center; margin-left: 5em }
-->
</STYLE>
```

The official CSS reference document is available online at http://www.w3.org/TR/REC-CSS1. It's a large document that is worth saving for offline reference

---

W3C   REC-CSS1-19990111

Cascading Style Sheets, level 1

W3C Recommendation 17 Dec 1996, revised 11 Jan 1999

This version:	http://www.w3.org/TR/1999/REC-CSS1-19990111
Latest version:	http://www.w3.org/TR/REC-CSS1
Previous version:	http://www.w3.org/TR/REC-CSS1-961217
Authors:	Håkon Wium Lie (howcome@w3.org)
	Bert Bos (bert@w3.org)

INTERMEDIATE: STYLESHEETS MADE SIMPLE

The code listing at the end of the previous page won't actually have a visible impact on the Web page when displayed in a browser, because it just defines the style. This means that in order to get some text displayed in that format, all that is needed is a reference to the style name, rather than a string of HTML tags.

So, when a Web browser comes across **<P CLASS="quotation">** somewhere in the HTML document, it will apply the style named 'quotation' to the following paragraph. Of course, paragraph tags are not the only way in which styles can be called up. They can be applied to most tags, including **<TR>** and **<TD>** tags, which will cause the contents of table rows or cells to be displayed according to the defined style.

Is this a dagger which I see before me,
The handle toward my hand? Come, let me clutch thee
I have thee not, and yet I see thee still.

INTERMEDIATE: STYLESHEETS MADE SIMPLE

Styles don't always have to be defined in the **<HEAD>** of a HTML document. This can be useful if you need to create an effect that is only used once, as it saves the nuisance of defining and then applying a style.

For example, to make a few words appear with a light blue background, simply use the code:
<SPAN STYLE="background: lightblue">Put some text here</SPAN>.

You probably aren't familiar with the **<SPAN>** tag, but suffice to say, it can be used to apply styles to non-structural sections of your HTML document. In this instance, we couldn't have used a **<P>** or even a **<DIV>** tag because the style needed to be applied in the middle of the sentence.

There I was, reading my Shakespeare, and suddenly it came, like a ██████████.

CHAPTER 14

INTERMEDIATE: YOU'VE BEEN FRAMED

INTERMEDIATE: YOU'VE BEEN FRAMED

Frames are an incredibly popular Web design feature, because they allow the browser window to be divided up into panes, each of which contains an independent HTML document. Although frames can cause all kinds of compatibility problems when done badly, when they're used correctly, they can be a speedy means of navigation. On top of this, there's always a dedicated **FRAMESET** file which defines the dimensions of the frames, and specifies which HTML pages should be loaded into each. This uses special HTML tags that you probably haven't come across before; an example is shown below.

```
<HTML>
<HEAD><TITLE>George the Goat's
Farmyard Frolics</TITLE></HEAD>
<FRAMESET ROWS="100,*">
<FRAME SRC="menu.html" NAME="above"
SCROLLING="NONE" NORESIZE
FRAMEBORDER="0">
<FRAME SRC="main.html" NAME="below"
SCROLLING="AUTO" NORESIZE
FRAMEBORDER="0">
</FRAMESET>
</HTML>
```

INTERMEDIATE: YOU'VE BEEN FRAMED

Now to explain the code from the last page. The **<TITLE>** tag won't appear on browsers that support frames, but should be included all the same. In the **FRAMESET** tag, you must specify either **ROWS** or **COLS** as the attribute. As used here, **ROWS** would divide the browser window into two horizontal sections, the first 100 pixels high and the other taking up all the remaining space on the screen.

The ***** symbol can be used more than once: the Web browser first works out what space is taken up by those frames with specific dimensions, and the remaining space is then divided equally between any ***** marked frames. **<FRAMESET ROWS = "50,*,*">** would make three frames, the second and third of equal vertical dimension (as shown in the example below.)

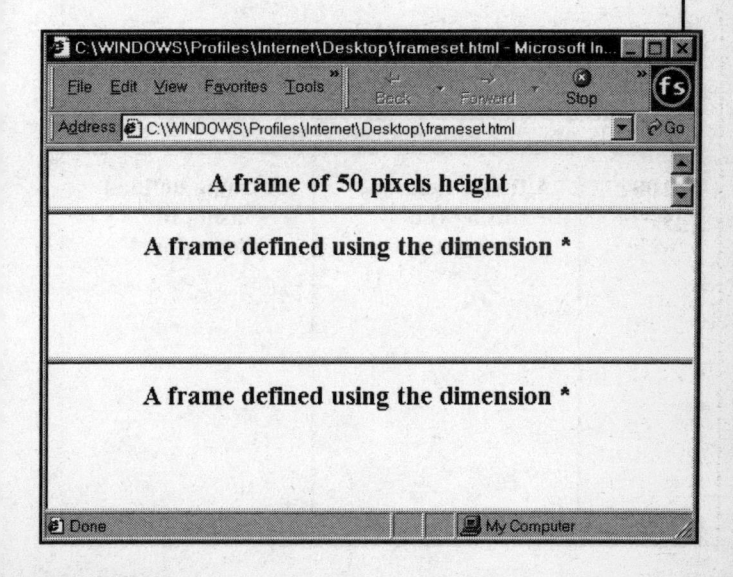

C:\WINDOWS\Profiles\Internet\Desktop\frameset.html - Microsoft In...

File   Edit   View   Favorites   Tools   Back   Forward   Stop

Address: C:\WINDOWS\Profiles\Internet\Desktop\frameset.html

A frame of 50 pixels height

A frame defined using the dimension *

A frame defined using the dimension *

Done — My Computer

INTERMEDIATE: YOU'VE BEEN FRAMED

The rules for dividing up the page into rows also applies to columns (or **COLS** in frameset tag lingo.) **<FRAMESET COLS = "100,*,*">** would produce three frames by dividing the browser window into columns, the first being 100 pixels wide and the other two of equal width, as illustrated below.

The **FRAMESET** tag should contain as many **FRAME** tags as there are frames. Each **FRAME** tag defines the HTML source, name and various other properties of the individual frames, and can contain the properties listed over the next two pages.

To place columns inside rows, or vice versa, then you just define the frameset as normal, and replace one of the **FRAME** tags with another **FRAMESET**, which must then contain its own **FRAME** tags. This is called 'nesting' of frames and an example is shown below.

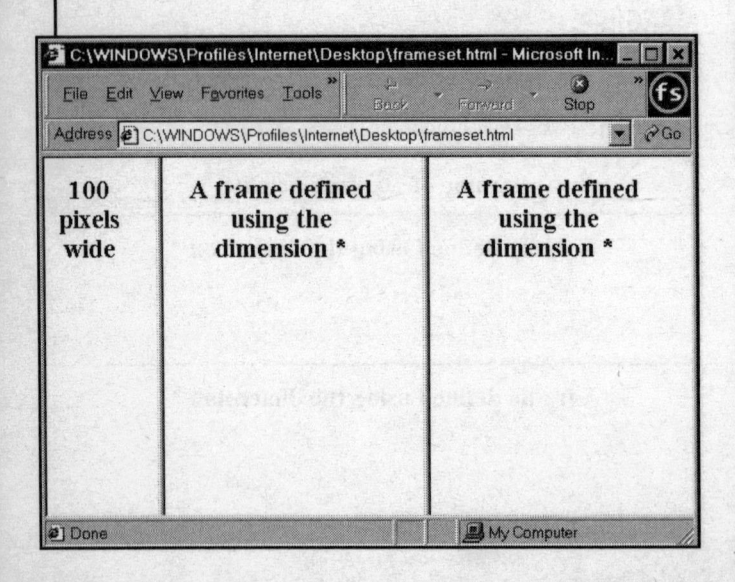

INTERMEDIATE: YOU'VE BEEN FRAMED

SRC
This is essential – it specifies which HTML page is to be placed in the frame. You can either choose to specify an exact URL – **http://www.mypage.com/myframe.html** or a relative one – **mypage.html**.

NAME
This is an optional property, which is useful if you need to link between frames. In the example below, the names relate logically to the position of the frames. Naming this way makes the names easier to remember.

MARGINWIDTH
Define this in pixels, eg: **MARGINWIDTH="5"**, to specify the width between frame edge and the start of the frame's contents.

MARGINHEIGHT
The same as **MARGINWIDTH**, but this controls the vertical gap between frame edge and the start of the frame's contents.

Get the full, official frame specification from
http://www.w3.org/TR/REC-html40/present/frames.html

---

previous   next   contents   elements   attributes   index

16 Frames

Contents

1. Introduction to frames
2. Layout of frames
    1. The FRAMESET element
        - Rows and columns
        - Nested frame sets
        - Sharing data among frames
    2. The FRAME element

SCROLLING
Can only be **AUTO**, **YES** or **NO**. Defines whether scrollbars should be placed at the frame's edge.

NORESIZE
Simply put this word into the **<FRAME>** tag to prevent the user from altering the size of the frames themselves. This guarantees that your design appears as you intended it.

FRAMEBORDER
Internet Explorer recognises this tag as a way of altering the gap between frames. Simply specify the desired size in pixels. To create a borderless frame, type **FRAMEBORDER = "0"**

BORDERCOLOR
Allows frame borders to be given their own colours, like page backgrounds. Specify the hexadecimal colour code required, eg **#FF0000** for red.

Get some hands-on advice on frames, plus a useful cheat sheet, at http://www.webreference.com/dev/frames/

---

home / web / dev / frames

Framing the Web

by Dan Brown (brown@greenonions.com)

Table of Contents

- Introduction
- The Layout <- Update! (borderless frames)
- Frame Interaction
- Getting Started
- Summary: Frames Cheat Sheet
- References <- Update!
- Appendix

INTERMEDIATE: YOU'VE BEEN FRAMED

As the screenshot below shows, the frameset code listed earlier works as soon as some dummy HTML files with the right names are created. But it needs refining. First of all, it needs to have some way of telling browsers that can't use frames what's going on. This is called the **NOFRAMES** tag, and can contain whatever text and HTML combination you want. Simply place something like this after the frameset:

```
<NOFRAMES><BODY>
<H1>Welcome to George the Goat's Farmyard
Frolics</H1>
You'll find out all about George's exciting life on the
farm at this site. Unfortunately your browser doesn't
support frames, but you can still navigate by following
this <A HREF="main.html">link</A> to the main
page.<P></BODY>
</NOFRAMES>
```

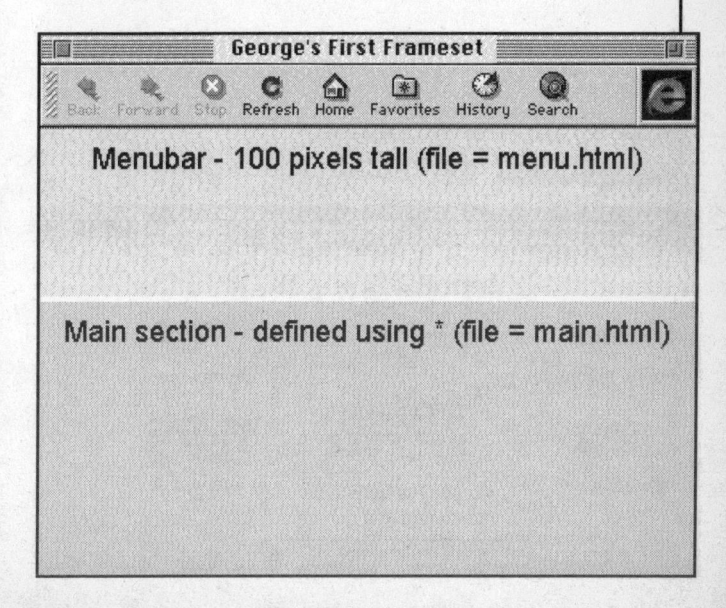

George's First Frameset

Menubar - 100 pixels tall (file = menu.html)

Main section - defined using * (file = main.html)

INTERMEDIATE: YOU'VE BEEN FRAMED

<u>As</u> mentioned in the description of the **FRAME** tag properties, it's possible to give each frame a name. This allows communication between these separate sections of the screen. If you've created a frameset with a navigation bar, then you'll probably want the links to make something load up in the main window.

This is devilishly simple – just add **TARGET="below"** to each of the links on the page. As the name of the main frame has been specified as **"below"** this will make the link load in that frame. Obviously, if you give a different name to your frames, then change the content of the **TARGET**.

Paragon Publishing's corporate site at http://paragon.co.uk/ makes use of frames, with all links from the navigation bar targeted at the main page area

INTERMEDIATE: YOU'VE BEEN FRAMED

To make life easier, it is possible to create a default target for all links on a HTML page. This means that navigation bars don't require each link to have a target declaration, unless the links needs to point to a frame other than the default one. Simply add **<BASE TARGET="below">** to the **<HEAD>** section of your HTML file.

One other use for the flexible **TARGET** attribute is to delete your frameset altogether. This is essential if you are linking to another site from your page. There really is nothing more annoying than a frameset that fails to budge. To do this, just put **TARGET = "_top"** in all links that go beyond your site, and be sure to use the underscore.

The Cool Site Of The Day site (http://cool.infi.net/) purposefully hangs on to its own frame system when sending users to recommended sites, so that they can give the page a rating

CHAPTER 15

INTERMEDIATE: FORM WITH FUNCTION

INTERMEDIATE: FORM WITH FUNCTION

Fill-in forms can be very useful for all kinds of Web design applications. The most common use is for simple fill-in forms, where Web site visitors are invited to leave their details. At their most complex, forms can be at the centre of an e-commerce site. And you're probably using forms more often than you realise. Whenever you select something from a pull-down menu on a Web site, you're using a form. With the advent of Javascript, forms are being used more than ever – there's more about this in Chapter 19.

To get you started with forms, this tutorial shows how to create a basic feedback form. The HTML shown below will create a simple form, with areas for name, email address and comments to be filled in.

```
<FORM
ACTION="mailto:james@paragon.co.uk"
METHOD="POST">
<PRE>
Name: <INPUT TYPE=text NAME="name">
Email: <INPUT TYPE=text NAME="email">
Comments:
<TEXTAREA NAME="comments"></TEXTAREA>
</PRE>
</FORM>
```

INTERMEDIATE: FORM WITH FUNCTION

So, just how does the form code shown on the opposite page work? The first line tells the browsers that the form is starting, and indicates which email address it should be sent to. Remember to replace the text in italics with your own email address.

The final part of this line lets the browser know exactly how to send the information – in the case of email, this is always going to be **POST**. The other **METHOD** options are only ever used with more complicated forms that involve server programming.

INTERMEDIATE: FORM WITH FUNCTION

Continuing with our look at the form code from the first page, **<PRE>** is a text styling tag which will help lay out forms easily. Every space and line return will be replicated in the browser window, unlike the normal configuration where a **
** or **<P>** tag is required.

The **<INPUT>** tag creates a small text box here, whereas **<TEXTAREA>** will generate a larger, scrolling box with more space for comments. Anything typed in between **<TEXTAREA>** and **</TEXTAREA>** will appear in this box when loaded into a Web browser.

The TEXTAREA tag is often used outside of the context of a form. Here it is used to cut down the space taken up by a large amount of text

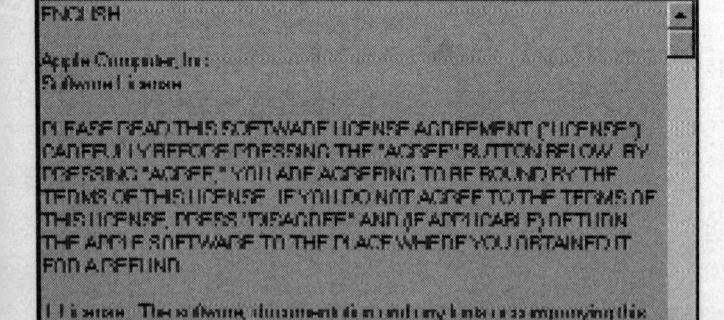

INTERMEDIATE: FORM WITH FUNCTION

The form is currently lacking two key components: the buttons which are needed to submit or clear the entry. These are defined using **<INPUT>** tags which are slightly different to the text box ones: **<INPUT TYPE=submit><INPUT TYPE=reset>**. Add this before the **</FORM>** tag.

All the functions of the form are now present, even if it is in a rather disorderly way. It is possible to tidy this up by specifying the size of the text boxes. For the small boxes, simply add **SIZE="40"** to the end of the **<INPUT>** tag and this will lock the width at 40 characters.

<TEXTAREA> tags can be edited to specify the size in terms of rows and columns. Add **ROWS="5" COLS="80" WRAP** to the end of the tag, and see what effect this has on the large text box by loading the HTML page into your Web browser. Notice that now you have added **WRAP** to the tag, automatic word wrap is active.

Test out your form by filling it in yourself and clicking the 'Submit' button. This may cause your browser to launch Outlook Express, which is an unfortunate tendency of recent Internet Explorer versions. The only solution to this problem is to avoid using mailto forms – alternatives are mentioned on the last page of this chapter.

But if your browser didn't launch Outlook Express, an email will soon arrive in your inbox, in a format that is very difficult to read – because the Web browser will have encoded the form before sending it on.

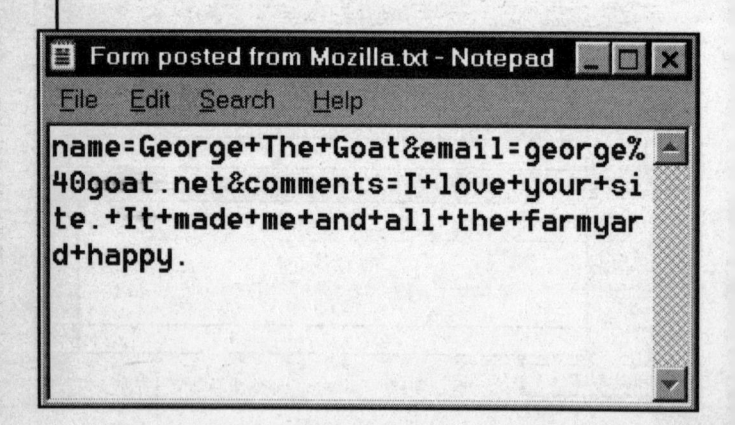

```
name=George+The+Goat&email=george%
40goat.net&comments=I+love+your+si
te.+It+made+me+and+all+the+farmyar
d+happy.
```

INTERMEDIATE: FORM WITH FUNCTION

The easiest solution to decoding the incoming email is to get hold of the URLcook shareware program, which is a tiny free download that takes encoded forms and converts them back into legible format. Visit **http://www.asan.com/users/therekutins/urlcook.html** to get your copy, and once installed follow the instructions below.

Bring up the encoded email on your screen, and select the text. Choose 'Copy' from the 'Edit' menu and then launch URLcook. Click the right mouse button anywhere in the top half of the window, and select 'Paste' from the pop-up menu that appears. Then click the Cook! button and somewhat more intelligible text will then appear.

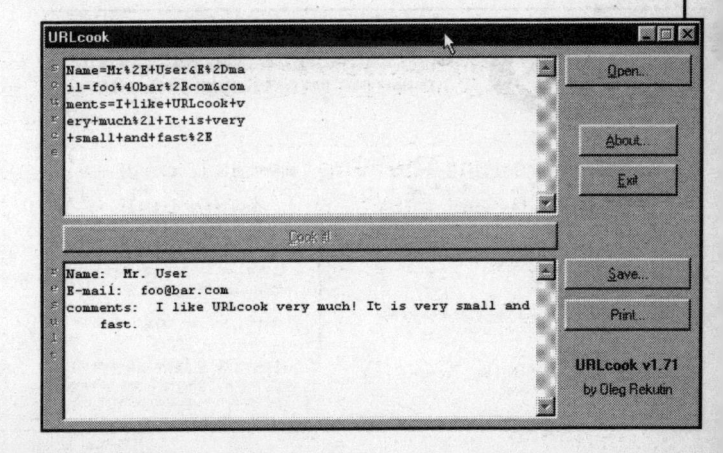

```
Name=Mr%2E+User&E%2Dma
il=foo%40bar%2Ecom&com
ments=I+like+URLcook+v
ery+much%21+It+is+very
+small+and+fast%2E
```

```
Name:  Mr. User
E-mail:  foo@bar.com
comments:  I like URLcook very much! It is very small and
    fast.
```

URLcook v1.71
by Oleg Rekutin

If you just want a guestbook service on your site, try signing up with a free service like Dreambook (**http://www.dreambook.com/**), which will automatically transfer your visitors' form input onto a custom guestbook page for you.

You could start putting a selection of user feedback on your home page, by simply transferring the output of WebParse into a HTML document. If you use a **<PRE>** tag around all of the comments, then you can get away with directly copying and pasting the URLcook output into your HTML document.

The **<PRE>** tag formats everything in monospaced type, and adds carriage returns where they appear in the HTML file (rather than requiring a **
** or **<P>**).

DREAMBOOK

Welcome to Dreambook, the free guest book service you've been dreaming about... from New Dream Network and Dreamhost.

- **make a book** — Create a Dreambook for your own website with our simple online system.
- **read a book** — Take a peek at a dreambook currently in use on a website.
- **change a book** — Change a dreambook that you have created.
- **book of help** — Need help? Confused? Click Here!

NEW Turn off the banner ads on your Dreambook! It's super-easy! For every site you host with Dreamhost you get one guestbook completely **ad-free**!

Companies can now advertise with Dream Book. For only $2 per 1,000 impressions, you can buy an advertising spot on over 240,000 guestbooks!

Go check out Dreamhost for reliable, inexpensive, high-quality site hosting. You can get yourname.com for only $9.95/month with no set up fee!

INTERMEDIATE: FORM WITH FUNCTION

Although this way of sending form information works fine for most of the time, it can also cause hassle with some browser configurations.

For example, if your visitor hasn't filled in their email server details, they will simply get an error message from their Web browser when they click 'Submit.' Also, recent Internet Explorer browsers seem to prefer launching Outlook Express to doing the form emailing work themselves.

If you want to get over this uncertainty of outcome, the easiest solution is to use the Response-o-Matic service at **http://www.response-o-matic.com/**, which gives you a free and simple means of getting all your form responses processed.

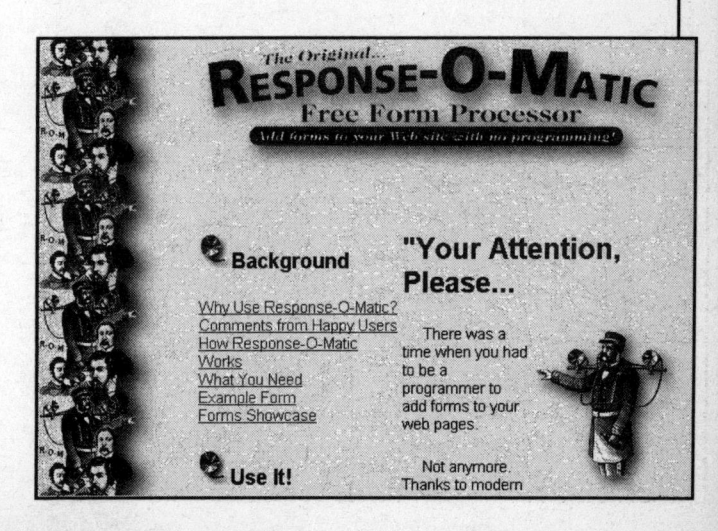

The Original...
RESPONSE-O-MATIC
Free Form Processor
Add forms to your Web site with no programming!

Background

Why Use Response-O-Matic?
Comments from Happy Users
How Response-O-Matic Works
What You Need
Example Form
Forms Showcase

Use It!

"Your Attention, Please...

There was a time when you had to be a programmer to add forms to your web pages.

Not anymore. Thanks to modern

CHAPTER 16

INTERMEDIATE: TABLES

INTERMEDIATE: TABLES

One of the biggest problems with designing Web pages is the lack of control you have over layout. Compared with the flexibility of desktop publishing, Web design is really still in the dark ages.

Although things have got a lot better in recent years – with the introduction of page layers and dynamic HTML – these advances are confusing and very complex. A simpler solution is to use tables, which are both versatile and easy to learn.

CNET's front page includes a total of 30 tables in its design, all seamlessly incorporated into one good-looking whole

INTERMEDIATE: TABLES

Tables allow you to tidy up your Web pages, putting images and text where you want them, while avoiding the use of frames, dynamic HTML and other satanic tools. Tables can be set up as 'invisible scaffolding' for your pages: you can set up their exact size in pixels, specify the number of rows and columns, change the background colour, and alter the spacing and alignment of cells.

This mini-tutorial will show you how to create a simple table. Try experimenting with setting your whole page in tables; this should keep the structure and design of the page clean and tidy.

Unsurprisingly, the main tag we're concerned with here is **<TABLE>**. A number of other tags must be nested within that tag to produce a functional table. Over the next few pages, all of the potential properties for these tags – ie, the configurable options that allow tables to be customised – are shown. After this, there's an example of how to put them into action.

Have a read of the official HTML specification for tables at
http://www.w3.org/TR/REC-html40/struct/tables.html

---

previous next contents elements attributes index

11 Tables

Contents

1. Introduction to tables
2. Elements for constructing tables
    1. The TABLE element
        - Table directionality
    2. Table Captions: The CAPTION element
    3. Row groups: the THEAD, TFOOT, and TBODY elements
    4. Column groups: the COLGROUP and COL elements
        - The COLGROUP element
        - The COL element
        - Calculating the number of columns in a table
        - Calculating the width of columns
    5. Table rows: The TR element

BGCOLOR

This controls the background colour of the table, row, or cell. It's a good idea to define a **BGCOLOR** for the whole table, which can optionally be altered by defining different ones in the **<TR>** and **<TD>** tags.

BORDER

Very important if you are working with 'invisible' tables, where **BORDER="0"** should be in the **<TABLE>** tag. Increasing the number gives a bevelled border around your tables. This can look dull, so try combining it with **CELLPADDING** and **CELLSPACING** (see below) to achieve different thicknesses and shading styles.

Extensive use of table background colours on this site (http://www.uk.bol.com/) makes it look visually appealing, without requiring too many images to be downloaded

INTERMEDIATE: TABLES

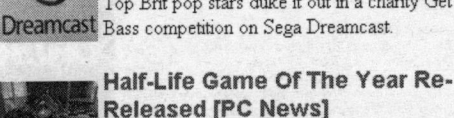

WIDTH can be specified in either pixels or percentage points. If you are unfamiliar with pixels, just remember that the average Web page is 550 to 600 pixels wide. Percentage points are most useful with **<TABLE>**, because it means that tables will resize with the browser window automatically. Fixed-width tables are increasingly common, because they ensure an integrity of design that percentage points cannot guarantee. Using **WIDTH** with **<TD>** is a good idea if you want to force the cell width to that size, although it will be changed if there is an image inside the cell that is wider.

Columns can have different widths specified, as shown here at http://totalgames.net/

INTERMEDIATE: TABLES

HEIGHT is often a useless notion in table design, because it depends on the number of lines needed for the text in the table – and all browsers will increase the size to fit everything in anyway. It can be useful, though, to force a larger cell or table height than would otherwise be allocated.

VALIGN Vertical alignment can be set as **TOP**, **MIDDLE** or **BOTTOM** – it simply places all the elements of the cell or row in question in the specified alignment.

ALIGN The cell or table row's contents can be arranged to the **LEFT**, **RIGHT** or **CENTER**. This can be changed by using the usual text or image alignment tags within the HTML of each cell.

This table from http://paragon.co.uk/ spans the entire page, and uses various ALIGN and VALIGN tags to put text and images in the right places

INTERMEDIATE: TABLES

CELLPADDING Give a number in pixels to get that much space between each cell's contents and its border.

CELLSPACING When a number is specified, that many pixels' spacing between cells is given by increasing the size of the border.

COLSPAN This cells to span more than one column. For example, you may have four evenly sized columns in the first row of the table. The second row could be split into two larger columns by using **COLSPAN=2** in each of the **<TD>** tags for the second row.

ROWSPAN Following the same principle as **COLSPAN**, it is also possible to have rows that span more vertical height than their counterparts.

This table, from the Practical Internet subscriptions page at http://pi.subs.net/, uses COLSPAN to extend the width of some cells, and ROWSPAN to control their height

INTERMEDIATE: TABLES

Although `<TABLE>` is the major tag, the sub-tags **`<TR>`** and **`<TD>`** are vital – they stand for Table Row and Table Data. TRs contain no data, they hold TDs, which separate data into individual cells.

Within these three tags, the properties of your table is set out bit by bit. I have put an example table together to demonstrate how it's done. The code is shown below, and the resulting table on the opposite page.

```
<TABLE BORDER=2 WIDTH="100%"
CELLPADDING="5" CELLSPACING="10"
BGCOLOR="#CCEEDD">
<TR><TD VALIGN="MIDDLE" ALIGN="CENTER">
<FONT SIZE="4">VAlign Middle<BR>Align
Center</FONT></TD>
<TD VALIGN="BOTTOM" ALIGN="RIGHT"
WIDTH="150" ROWSPAN="2">
<FONT SIZE="4">VAlign Bottom<BR>Align
Right<BR>Rowspan 2</FONT></TD></TR>
<TR><TD HEIGHT="100" VALIGN="MIDDLE"
ALIGN="full">
<FONT SIZE="4">Height 100<BR>VAlign
Middle<BR>Align Center</FONT></TD></TR>
<TR><TD COLSPAN="2" BGCOLOR="#FFFFBB">
<FONT SIZE="4">Colspan 2<BR>BGColor
#FFFFBB</FONT></TD></TR>
</TABLE>
```

INTERMEDIATE: TABLES

This table shows which tag can house the different properties shown. Only the tags needed to build your particular table design need to be included in the HTML of your page.

	`<TABLE>`	`<TR>`	`<TD>`
BGCOLOR	Yes	Yes	Yes
BORDER	Yes	No	No
WIDTH	Yes	No	Yes
HEIGHT	Yes	Yes	Yes
VALIGN	No	Yes	Yes
ALIGN	No	Yes	Yes
CELLPADDING	Yes	No	No
CELLSPACING	Yes	No	No
COLSPAN	No	No	Yes
ROWSPAN	No	Yes	No

VAlign Middle Align Center

Height 100 VAlign Middle Align Center

VAlign Bottom Align Right Rowspan 2

Colspan 2 BGColor #FFFFBB

INTERMEDIATE: PREPARING GRAPHICS

CHAPTER 17

INTERMEDIATE: PREPARING GRAPHICS

Learn how to prepare a graphic for your site using Paint Shop Pro 5 (available from http://www.jasc.com/), and then find out how to place it in your HTML code

INTERMEDIATE: PREPARING GRAPHICS

Step One First you have to put the picture into a format that can be viewed on a computer – a process known as digitising. Digitise an image by scanning it with a scanner, or by photographing it with a digital camera. Once you have digitised your picture, you need to open it in Paint Shop Pro using the 'Open' command from the 'File' menu. When the image is open in Paint Shop Pro, notice that there is a vertical line of editing tools running down the left-hand side. They look rather esoteric, but you can find out which icon does what by pointing your cursor at the icon. A little text box reveals its function – the tool here crops images, for example.

INTERMEDIATE: PREPARING GRAPHICS

Step Two You may want to crop the most important part of the image, cutting away the background so it has more impact on your Web page. Here, we have cropped out Rosie's head and shoulders by selecting this area with the Crop tool and then double-clicking. Blurry images won't look very good on your Web site, so if a picture is a little hazy, you can sharpen it up. Go to the 'Image' menu and click on the 'Sharpen' option. If the image is badly blurred, however, this won't help much. You'll have to re-digitise the image or use an alternative one.

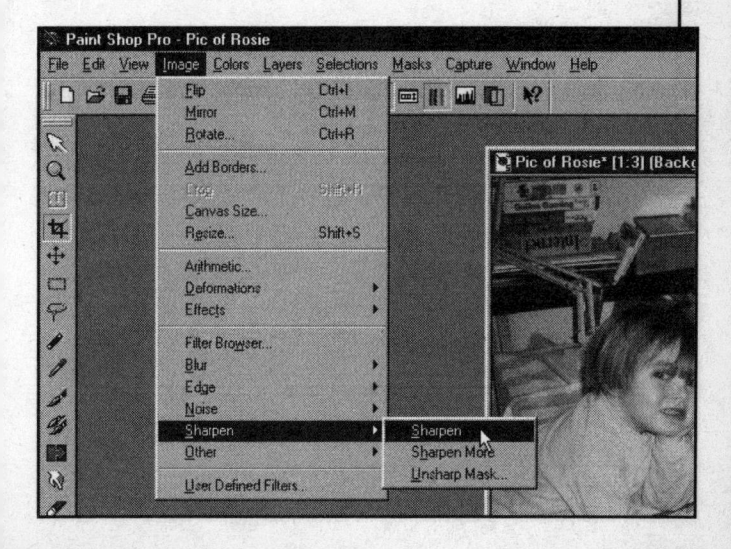

INTERMEDIATE: PREPARING GRAPHICS

Step Three Retouching the image can also be done quite easily. Select the 'Retouch' tool from the left-hand toolbar and then click the left mouse button in the part of the image that you want to retouch. When working with the editing tools, don't forget the Zoom function (a little magnifying glass). This allows you to work in great detail. Every time you click the magnifying glass, you zoom in further. To zoom back out, just click the right mouse button.

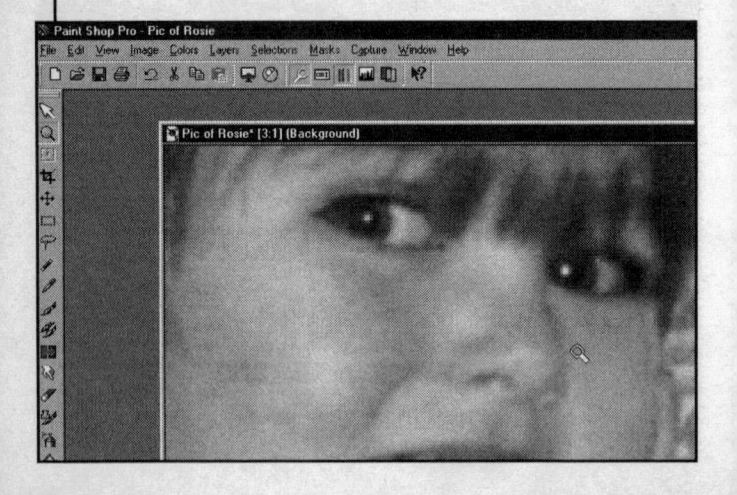

INTERMEDIATE: PREPARING GRAPHICS

Step Four
Now we've done some very simple editing, it's time to prepare the picture for going on our Web site. For a photograph like this, we are going to save the image as a JPEG file. This ensures the quality is as high as possible while the file size stays low. With the picture open, go to the File menu, select 'Save as' and then 'JPEG.' Don't save just yet. Click on 'Options' and select the button 'Progressive encoding.' This will cause the image to download in stages, which is better than keeping visitors to your site waiting around for the picture to come through all at once. Now save the image.

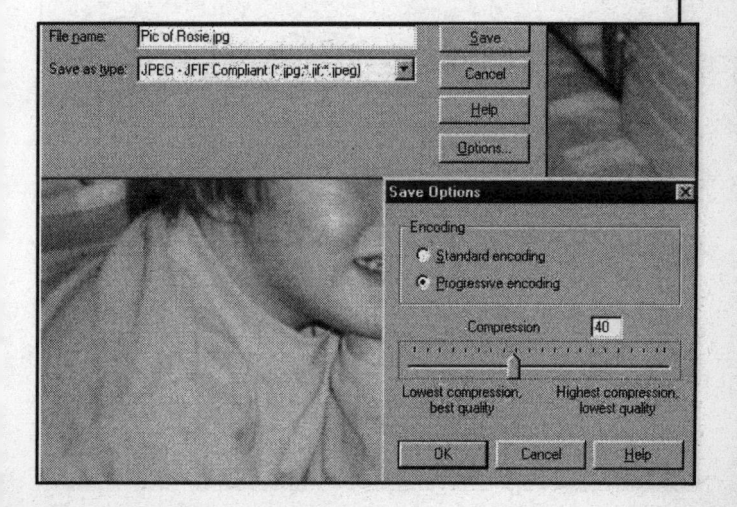

INTERMEDIATE: PREPARING GRAPHICS

Step Five The image dimensions are still too large. Go to the 'Image' menu and click 'Resize' to fix this. We reduce the Width and Height percentage sizes by a third, entering the new values in the relevant boxes. Ensure 'Smart Size' is selected as the Resize Type and click 'OK.' Almost there. To give a final check to your image, open it with your Web browser. Go to the File menu, select 'Open' and click your way through the boxes so your Web browser opens the file from your hard drive rather than trying to open a Web site. In Navigator, you need to select 'All Files' from the pull-down menu before it sees the file.

INTERMEDIATE: PREPARING GRAPHICS

Step Six To incorporate an image – now a rather fetching fish – into the HTML on your Web site, you need to use the **<IMG>** tag first mentioned in Chapter Four. In its most simple form, it defines the location where the desired image can be found. If I wanted to use an image called fish.gif in the images directory, then the simplest tag needed would be **<IMG SRC="images/fish.gif">**. That may sound simple enough, but it is actually a detailed procedure – your browser still needs to know what size the image is going to be, where it should be placed on the page, what the image depicts, and whether it should have a border, spacing, or an imagemap attached.

The effect of specifying TOP as the ALIGN value. See step eight

INTERMEDIATE: PREPARING GRAPHICS

Step Seven To let the Web browser know in advance what size your image is, the **WIDTH** and **HEIGHT** properties are essential. It is important to find out the exact size of your image, as there is nothing worse than re-sizing graphics using the **WIDTH** and **HEIGHT** tags: it is bad practice, and tends to look awful. Netscape Navigator will tell you the size of any image if you load it into the Web browser window. The pixel size will then be displayed in the menu bar. Explorer users can find out by checking the 'Properties,' accessed by right-clicking on the image. Our HTML tag now reads **<IMG SRC="images/fish.gif" ALT="Fooey the Fish" WIDTH="200" HEIGHT="234">**.

This is what happens when you have RIGHT as the ALIGN value. See step eight

Fooey the Fish

Fooey (famed fish) frolicks frenetically from France for Folkestone forgetting fortuitously forfeited fishcakes for feeding from.

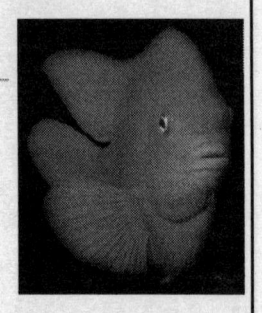

INTERMEDIATE: PREPARING GRAPHICS

Step Eight Spacing is a useful feature, as it allows the image to be given extra white space in horizontal (**HSPACE**) and vertical (**VSPACE**) dimensions. Adding **HSPACE="5" VSPACE="10"** to the tag gives 5 pixels extra spacing to the left and right of the image, and 10 pixels extra above and below it. The final property which I will look at is the most important of all – **ALIGN**. If an alignment hasn't been specified, an image gets thrown into the text like an oversized character. This can look pretty bad, and may be interpreted differently between browsers. The options for the **ALIGN** property are **TOP**, **MIDDLE**, **BOTTOM**, **LEFT** and **RIGHT**.

This is what happens when you have MIDDLE as the ALIGN value

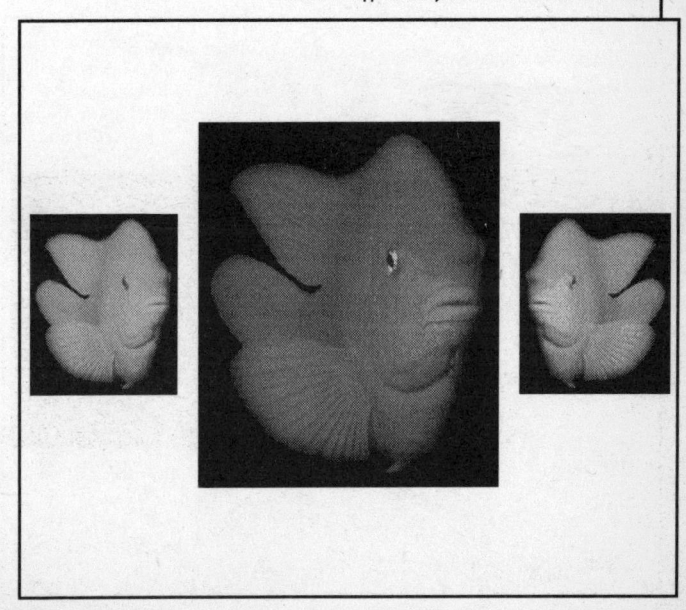

CHAPTER 18

ADVANCED: IMAGEMAPS

ADVANCED: IMAGEMAPS

One of the most common means of providing quick navigation around a site is through the use of a button bar that is hotlinked by an imagemap. In the bad old days of the Web, these had to be handled 'server-side' with the co-ordinates of the user's click being passed back to the Web server for it to decide where to send them next. Whilst it is still possible to use this method, virtually all Web browsers now support client-side imagemaps. This is where the HTML contains the map co-ordinates, and it is the Web browser itself that decides where the user should be sent based on the location of their click. This tutorial will take you through creating a client-side imagemap of your own.

Paragon Internet's site at http://www.pinet.co.uk/ uses an imagemap on its front page. Note that text links are also provided to retain compatibility with older browsers

ADVANCED: IMAGEMAPS

Step One Open your button bar design in your graphic design package of choice (eg Paint Shop Pro or whatever package you created it in). If you haven't yet made a button bar, do this first so that you've got something to work with in this tutorial. Decide which of the areas of the button bar you wish to have links in and write them down on a piece of paper. You will soon need to note down the co-ordinates for each area that is hotlinked. You need to have your graphics software show you the co-ordinates of where the mouse pointer is, a function normally found in the 'Info' palette (or possibly integrated in part of the window design). This is essential, as you must have accurate co-ordinates.

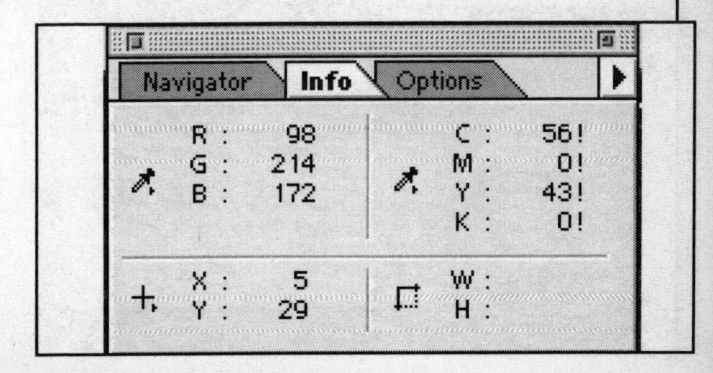

ADVANCED: IMAGEMAPS

Step Two Move your mouse pointer to the top left-hand corner of the image. The co-ordinate readout should show 0,0 (or something close to that). Some paint packages use other origins for their co-ordinates, but all imagemaps are based on 0,0 being the top left-hand corner. If this isn't the case with your package, compensate by rotating or flipping the graphic so that what is normally the top-left corner is positioned at the 0,0 point. Decide which of the areas of the button bar you wish to have linked, and write them down on a piece of paper. You will soon need to note down the co-ordinates for each area that is hotlinked.

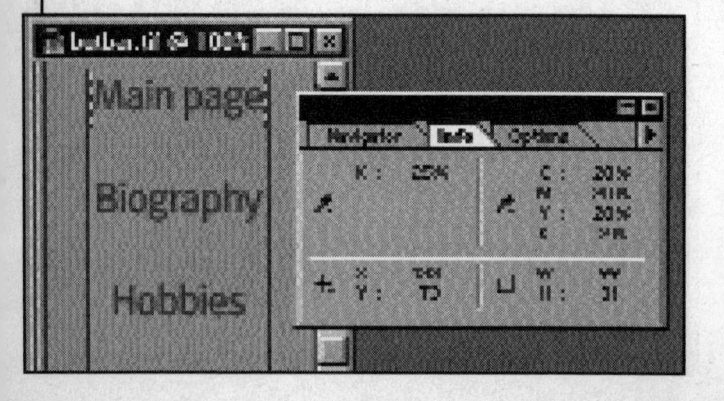

ADVANCED: IMAGEMAPS

Step Three Move your mouse to the top-left corner of the first area that needs to be hotlinked. Note down the co-ordinates of this location, taking the X co-ordinate first. Then move the mouse to the bottom right-hand corner of the area in question. Note down these co-ordinates. Imagemap co-ordinates are based on the top-left and bottom-right positions only, with 0,0 being the top left-hand corner of the whole button bar image.

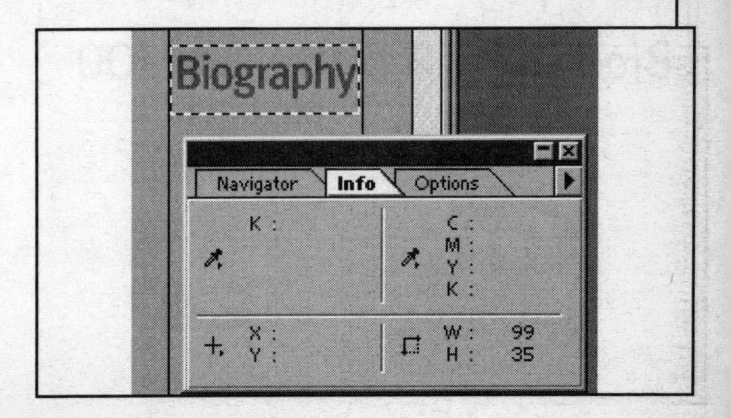

ADVANCED: IMAGEMAPS

Step Five Repeat step three for all the areas of the image that need to be linked up. With the sample button bar that's described below, you'll find that the regular pattern will make it easier to work out the co-ordinates. The starting X co-ordinate is always 0 and the final X co-ordinate is always 100 (the width of the image in pixels). When you have completed recording your co-ordinates, you should have written down something resembling the text below.

Main page 0,0 to 100,50
Biography 0,50 to 100,100

ADVANCED: IMAGEMAPS

Step Six Close your graphics package, and open up the HTML file that will contain the button bar. If you just want to test the imagemap, then create a dummy HTML file instead with just the bare **<HTML>**, **<HEAD>**, **<TITLE>** and **<BODY>** tags. In the **<HEAD>** section of the HTML file, enter this code:
  <MAP NAME="buttonbar">
  </MAP>

For each area that needs to be linked, you should add a line like this between the **<MAP>** and **</MAP>** tags: **<AREA TYPE=RECT COORDS="0,0,100,50" HREF="index.html">** Obviously, you need to replace the co-ordinates with your own, and the HREF should point to the page that will appear after clicking that area of the image. Note that co-ordinates are entered as four numbers separated by commas. The finished **<MAP>** for the sample button bar is shown below.

```
<MAP NAME="buttonbar">
<AREA TYPE=RECT COORDS="0,0,100,50"
HREF="index.html">
<AREA TYPE=RECT COORDS="0,50,100,100"
HREF="biog.html">
<AREA TYPE=RECT COORDS="0,100,100,150"
HREF="hobbies.html">
<AREA TYPE=RECT COORDS="0,150,100,200"
HREF="links.html">
<AREA TYPE=RECT COORDS="0,200,100,250"
HREF="contact.html">
<AREA TYPE=RECT COORDS="10,280,45,300"
HREF="mailto:james@paragon.co.uk">
<AREA TYPE=RECT COORDS="45,280,65,300"
HREF="http://www.icq.com/">
<AREA TYPE=RECT COORDS="65,280,90,300"
HREF="http://www.aol.com/">
</MAP>
```

ADVANCED: IMAGEMAPS

Step Seven The final three **<AREA>** tags are for the 'QuickLinks' section at the bottom of the sample button bar, and could be changed so that clicking 'ICQ' links to an ICQ personal page, and clicking AOL links to Instant Messenger or a page at **http://members.aol.com**. These are just to show that you're not completely stuck with local links; in fact, you can send emails using them, as is shown with the mailto link above. Now you need to enter the code to make the button bar appear, which is simply a glorified **<IMG>** tag: **<IMG SRC="buttonbar.gif" WIDTH="100" HEIGHT="300" BORDER="0" USEMAP="#buttonbar">**

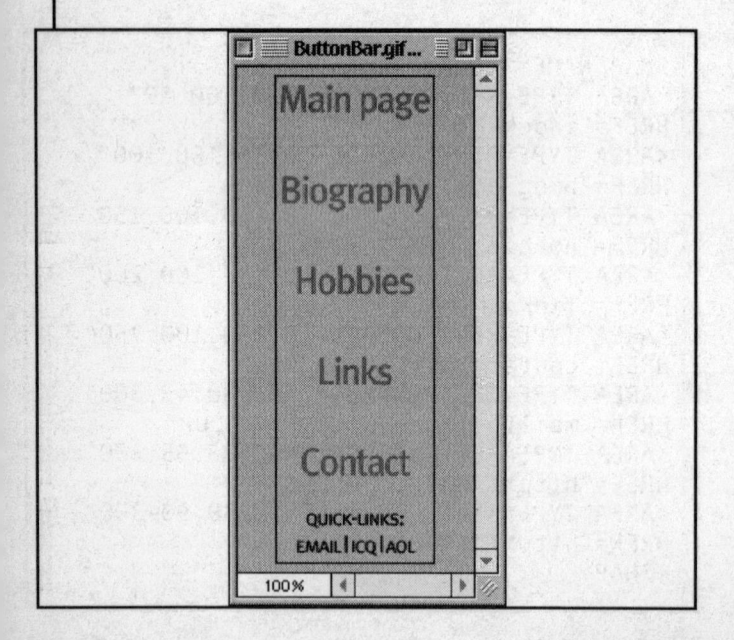

ADVANCED: IMAGEMAPS

Step Eight You need to change the **SRC**, **WIDTH** and **HEIGHT** from the code provided here to fit your own image's location and dimensions. The **USEMAP** refers to the **<MAP>** created in the **<HEAD>** of the HTML. The hash (#) in front of the name is essential. Save the HTML file and load it into your Web browser. Wave your mouse cursor over the image and check that the hotspots are correct, and link to the correct pages elsewhere on your site. If it does, you could always use the imagemap across your entire site as the standard navigation bar.

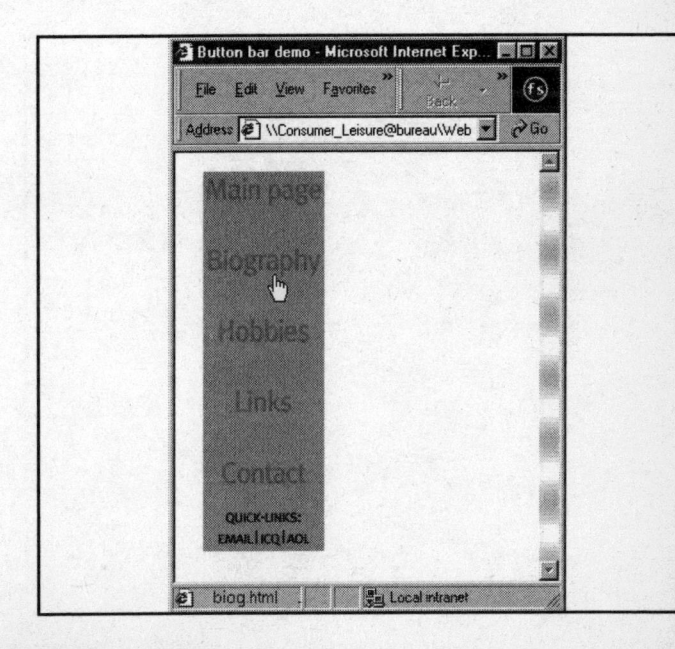

CHAPTER 19

ADVANCED: SCRIPTING SENSATION

ADVANCED: SCRIPTING SENSATION

Step One One of the simplest but most effective navigational tools is the pull-down menu. All users are familiar with this, as they resemble the menus used in operating systems such as Windows to execute commands. The normal problem is that pull-down menus only activate when a 'Submit' button is clicked, as they are part of a form that has to be submitted for it to do anything. With a little sprinkling of simple Javascript, this step can be avoided. If you're not interested in the innards of the Javascript, then you could just type the code snippet below into the **<HEAD>** section of your HTML and not worry about how it works.

```
<SCRIPT LANGUAGE=JavaScript>
<!--
function goClick() {
var URL =
document.browse.picker.options[document.
browse.picker.selectedIndex].value;
top.location.href = URL;
}
// -->
</SCRIPT>
```

ADVANCED: SCRIPTING SENSATION

Step Two Let's explain the Javascript anyway, for those readers who have an interest in such things. The function part of the script is encased in curly brackets, and is called goClick. The line beginning var brings the destination Web address for the selected menu item into a usable form, by storing it in a variable called URL. The first part (**document.browse.picker.options**) points to the pull-down menu's range of available options, and the bit in square brackets points to the selected menu item. Document is a Javascript term that shows we are talking about something to do with the document on screen at the present time; browse is the name of the form being used; picker is the name of the pull-down menu.

Netscape's Page Info command is useful for tracking the structure of documents – which is essential for Javascripting

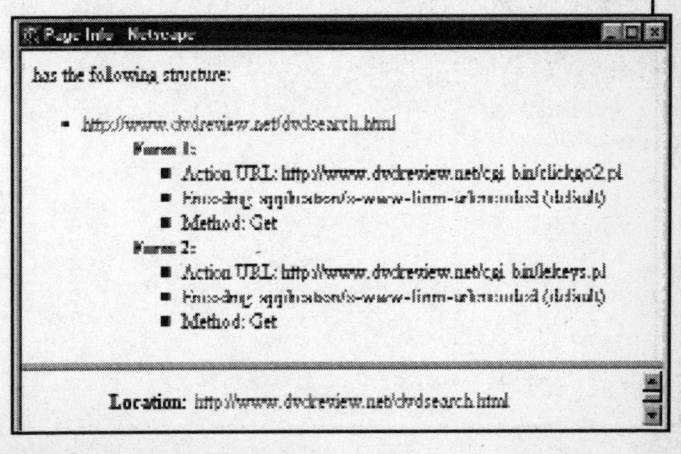

Page Info - Netscape

has the following structure:

- http://www.dvdreview.net/dvdsearch.html
    - **Form 1:**
        - Action URL: http://www.dvdreview.net/cgi-bin/clickgo2.pl
        - Encoding: application/x-www-form-urlencoded (default)
        - Method: Get
    - **Form 2:**
        - Action URL: http://www.dvdreview.net/cgi-bin/fekeys.pl
        - Encoding: application/x-www-form-urlencoded (default)
        - Method: Get

Location: http://www.dvdreview.net/dvdsearch.html

ADVANCED: SCRIPTING SENSATION

Step Three In effect, this tracks down the particular part of the document by working down the hierarchy from the whole page, to a specific form, to the pull-down menu in that form, and then the chosen option in that pull-down menu. Most crucial of all, 'value' on the end shows that we are looking for the **VALUE** of the selected **OPTION**, which is in fact the URL of the destination page. The next line tells the browser to move to the URL that has just been tracked down, and is the only part of the script with an ultimate visible effect that the user will notice.

ADVANCED: SCRIPTING SENSATION

Step Four We will now create the pull-down menu, which is used to trigger the script. All pull-down menus must be part of a HTML form, and for the purposes of the Javascript we must name the form browse. Add this line to your HTML code, in the position where the menu is to appear: **<FORM NAME="browse">** Now to create the menu using the **<SELECT>** tag. Again, we must match the name of the menu to the value given in the Javascript. More importantly, we need to include a little nugget of Javascript in the tag itself to trigger the goClick function whenever the menu is changed. All of this is done with one magic line of code: **<SELECT NAME="picker" onChange="goClick()">**

Step Five
Within the **<SELECT>** tag, **<OPTION>** tags specify the menu items. The most important property of concern to us is **VALUE**, where the destination URL will be specified. For the first option, we will just specify the index page, because it is not a real destination – it is just the title of the menu. Note that even with blank menu items (often used to split up a long menu) you must include some **VALUE** or a JavaScript error will occur. Enter the code **<OPTION SELECTED VALUE="index.html">QuickMenu</OPTION>**.

ADVANCED: SCRIPTING SENSATION

Step Six
Now we can add as many further **<OPTION>** tags as required, with one for each menu item. You should add one for each page on your site: **<OPTION VALUE="page1.html"> First page </OPTION>**. Once you have all of the menu options specified, close off the menu and the form with these tags: **</SELECT> </FORM>**. Save the page and view it in a Web browser. With any joy, if you select an option, it should move to the page specified in the HTML code. If it fails to work, then check that you have Javascript enabled and double check to make sure you have entered the code correctly.

ADVANCED: SCRIPTING SENSATION

Step Seven Anything involving Javascript can come unstuck for a number of reasons, especially those involving old browsers and bizarre implementations of the scripting language. It is in fact possible to adapt the above framework, to work with non-JavaScript browsers. By cunning use of a CGI script called ClickGo, available from **http://www.staff.net/cgi-scripts/**, together with the **<NOSCRIPT>** tag, this makes the navigation system fairly immune from problems of incompatibility. The method described on the opposite page isn't for the faint-hearted, and comes with apologies to the authors of ClickGo.

ADVANCED: SCRIPTING SENSATION

Step Eight
Add **ACTION="http://path/to/clickgo.pl" METHOD="GET"** to your **<FORM>** tag. Add **<NOSCRIPT><INPUT TYPE=SUBMIT VALUE="Go!"></NOSCRIPT>** before the **</FORM>** tag. Download ClickGo and open it in a text editor. Look for the text "goto" and change it to "picker." Save the script and upload it to the CGI-BIN of your Web server. Turn off Javascript in your Web browser, open the modified HTML file, and you should see a button next to the menu. Select an option, click the button, and you should be transported to the correct URL. But be careful to specify full URLs in all the **VALUE** properties when using this system!

CHAPTER 20

ADVANCED: SOUNDING OFF

ADVANCED: SOUNDING OFF

Step One Designing a Web page isn't just about text and graphics. If you want to tap into the enormous potential of multimedia content for your site, then it's a good idea to start at the ground floor by adding some sounds. This is much easier than you might think, both in terms of getting the sound that you want recorded and then adding it to your page. If you're using Windows, then all of the software you'll need is included in your standard installation. Take a look at the 'Accessories' section of the 'Programs' listing of your 'Start' menu. There is a section called 'Multimedia', which is shown in the screenshot below.

ADVANCED: SOUNDING OFF

Step Two To record your sound, you'll need to launch the Sound Recorder program (Start Menu > Programs > Accessories > Multimedia). The start-up screen for this program is shown below. Before starting on the recording, you need to set up the sound source. Basically, you'll need to plug in the sound source to the microphone or line input of your sound card. If you are recording your own voice, then just plug the microphone you're using into the port. Tape or CD sources can also be plugged in by using an audio cable to link their earphone socket and the sound card.

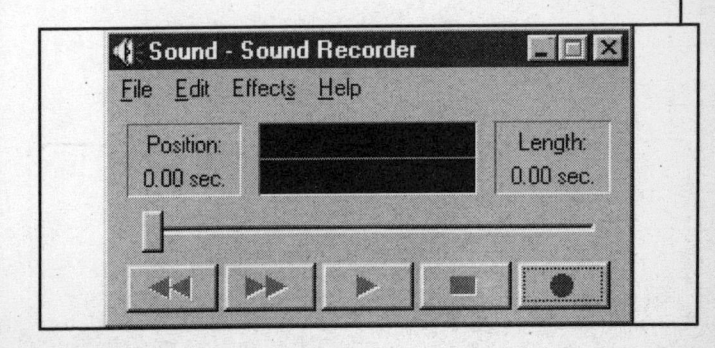

ADVANCED: SOUNDING OFF

Step Three To configure Sound Recorder for your desired settings, go to the Audio Properties item in the Edit menu. This will show the screen below. Using the pop-up menu labelled 'Preferred device' under the 'Recording' heading, select your sound card. Depending on the exact model of card you are using, the options will differ. Then set the quality of the recording by selecting 'Radio' from the 'Preferred quality' menu. You can also alter the volume using this slider on this control panel. For the moment, leave the volume as it is – but if the recording is too quiet or too loud, come back and make the necessary adjustment. Click on 'OK' when you want to confirm the chosen settings.

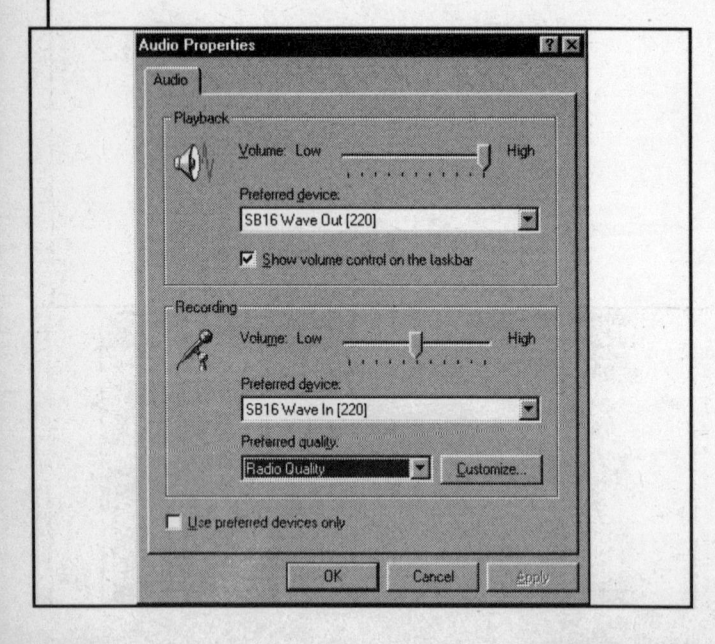

ADVANCED: SOUNDING OFF

Step Four Now that you're back to the main Sound Recorder display, you can start recording. You need to be very precise about starting the recording at the right time. When you're ready, click the red circle (record) button. To stop recording, click the black square (stop) button. Play back the sound once it's recorded by clicking the black triangle (play) button. Leave your computer speakers at their normal volume. If the sound volume needs altering, use the relevant commands in the 'Effects' menu shown below. Excessive use of this feature degrades quality, so be sure to listen to the sound after applying effects.

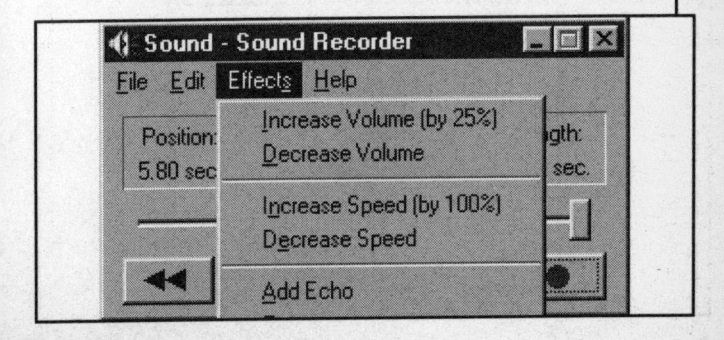

ADVANCED: SOUNDING OFF

Step Five To save the sound file, simply select 'Save' from the 'File' menu. Ensure that the file format selected is WAV. Place the file in the same folder as the other files used for your Web site. Check the size of the sound file by opening your Web site directory on the Windows desktop, and clicking once on its icon. In the bottom right-hand section of the window, the size of the sound file will be displayed. This sound has a file size of 125k, which is reasonable for downloading over a modem connection. Try and keep sounds under 300k as a general rule.

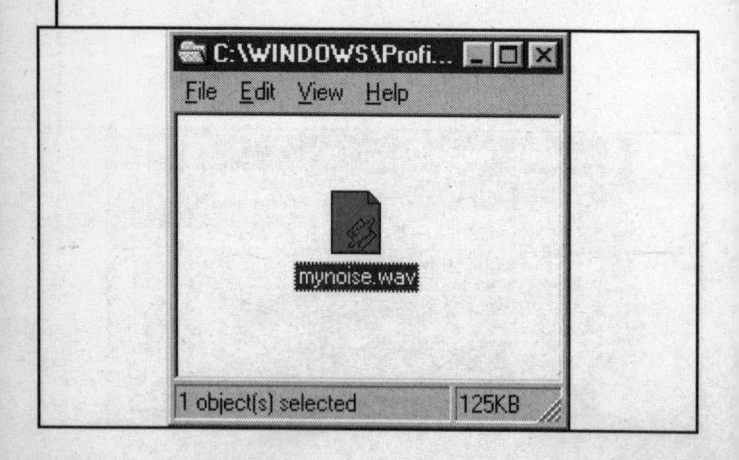

ADVANCED: SOUNDING OFF

Step Six To incorporate the sound into your Web page, simply add a standard hypertext link. For example,

<A HREF="mynoise.wav">Click here to listen to mynoise.wav</A>

The exact reaction of the user's Web browser depends heavily on whether they are using Explorer, Navigator or something else. Extra applications such as WinAmp may also meddle with the plug-in or helper application used to play the sound file, although Navigator tends to consistently launch its own Java-based sound playing tool, as shown below.

ADVANCED: SOUNDING OFF

Step Seven Getting the sound played is the weak link in the chain, although you can be fairly sure that anyone clicking on the hyperlink will either hear the sound straight away, or be offered the option to save it on their hard disk for later playing. If you don't achieve the desired results with recording your own sounds, it might be a good idea to pay a visit to **http://www.favewavs.com/**. This site has hundreds of freely downloadable sounds files available, which can be easily incorporated in your Web pages.

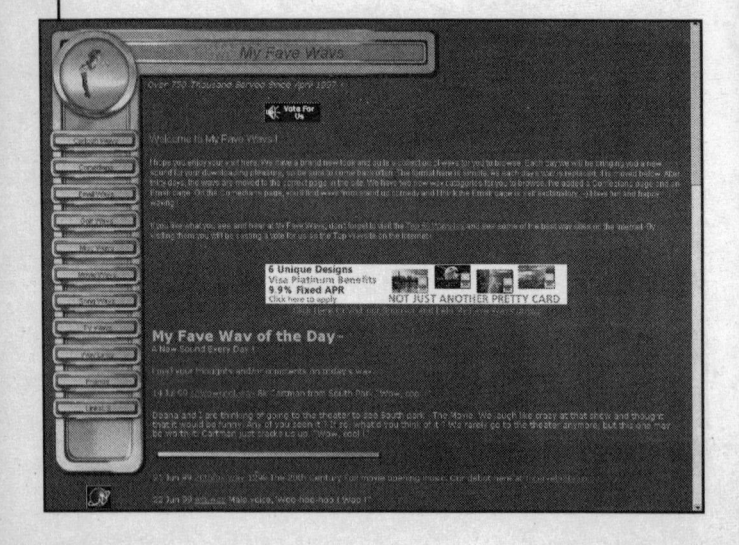

ADVANCED: SOUNDING OFF

Step Eight WAV is the standard Windows sound format, and is therefore the best bet for projects of this kind where maximum compatibility is a big issue. However, you'll no doubt be aware of the existence of MP3 audio files, which, as well as sounding great, offer much more efficient compression and can be streamed – which means they are played during downloading. You don't have to wait for the entire jobby to come down your phone line. More information and relevant software tools can be found at the site shown below, **http://www.mp3.com/**. If you use this format, restrict their use to longer sound effects that would be too large to present as WAV files to the user.

CHAPTER 21

ADVANCED: BEEFED-UP BROWSER

Find out about some of the latest technologies that can be used to beef-up your Web pages

ADVANCED: BEEFED-UP BROWSER

Java palaver
Java is a very tricky issue, especially considering the wide gulf between the marketing claims about Java, and how it actually 'feels' for the end user. Java is especially slow on Macintosh machines, and things aren't much better with Windows. The other issue to consider is that Java is very difficult to code for yourself. If you are planning to use pre-written applets that are available online, this is often a fairly futile exercise. Most free applets will produce an effect or perform a function that is done better by some other Internet technology.

Java was first launched by Sun way back in 1995. Catch up on the latest news from them at http://www.java.sun.com/

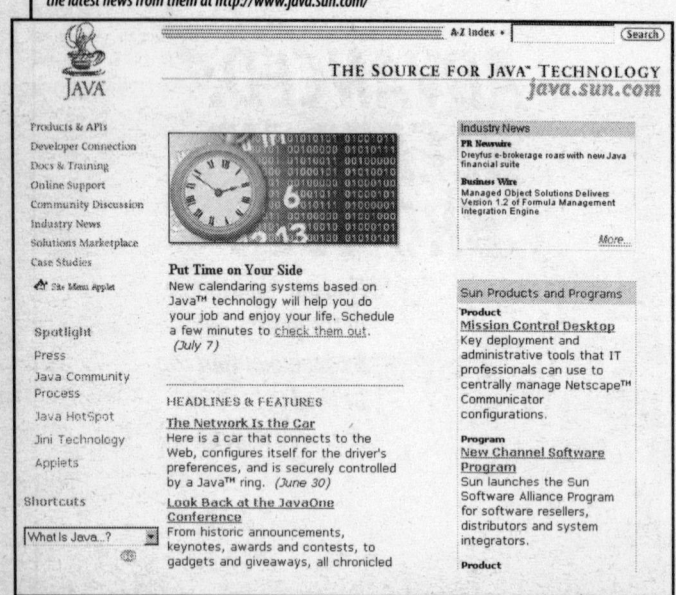

ADVANCED: BEEFED-UP BROWSER

Java was introduced back in 1995, when animated GIFs weren't supported by browsers and sound files simply didn't come into the Web surfing equation. Now that these technologies are available, there's really no point in using Java applets to produce audio-visual effects that can be replicated using faster methods. One of the original showcase Java applets that Sun used on its home page a few years ago did nothing other than animate images and play sounds according to the position of the mouse on the page. It simply doesn't make sense anymore to use Java in this way.

Shockwave & Flash : they were but twinkles in the eyes of Macromedia (http://www.shockwave.com/) back when Java was launched. But now they often present easier and quicker ways of producing audiovisual effects

ADVANCED: BEEFED-UP BROWSER

Whilst Java is an impressive language in some ways, to use it to best effect you need to be a programming expert with a better reason to deploy an applet in a Web page than animating an image. If you're interested in seeing how Java is being put to work at the moment, a good place to start is the Java Applet Rating System (JARS) at **http://www.jars.com/**. Many popular sites put Java to good use, such as the BBC News site at **http://news.bbc.co.uk/**, which has a news ticker on its front page powered by a Java applet.

ADVANCED: BEEFED-UP BROWSER

Perl of wisdom

With the introduction of JavaScript to the Web scene in the last couple of years, more traditional server-side scripting languages seem to have been pushed aside in favour of the client-side approach. This is despite the fact that scripts residing on the server can perform many more functions and produce much more impressive and consistent results than even the most well-formed Javascript. Perhaps the easiest route into server-side scripting is Perl. Created by Larry Wall, this scripting language was designed mainly for working with text operations, especially those that involved processing textual input into a different form.

Perl's founding father Larry Wall has written books about the language for publishers O'Reilly, who have a site dedicated to Perl at http://perl.oreilly.com/

ADVANCED: BEEFED-UP BROWSER

What does all of this mean to the humble home page creator? Well, it basically means that you can vastly improve the sheen of your site through writing Perl scripts which make it interactive or user-customisable in a way that isn't possible with Javascript. Because Perl runs from the Web server side of things, it can store, recall and change files on the server. This make the results more reliable, because the script is processed by the server rather than the user's browser. So Perl is the ideal solution for scripting projects that need to call on data files.

Find out about Javascript by paying a visit to www.webcoder.com. Tutorials on dynamic HTML are also available at this site

ADVANCED: BEEFED-UP BROWSER

For example, if you're creating a script to search your site or list items in a database, then Perl definitely wins over Javascript. However, you'd be better off opting for Javascript if you don't need access to server-based data files, and you can live with the slight unpredictability of Javascript being processed by the user's Web browser instead of your Web server.

In fact, you may find that the best solution involves mixing the two scripting languages to maximise their potential. This was the approach adapted at **http://www.dvdreview.net/**, where a Perl-powered shopping cart and search engine is complemented by Javascript-based navigation systems.

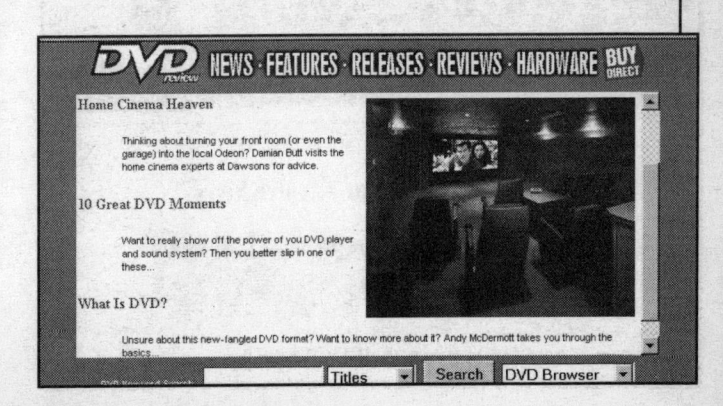

There's not enough space to go into the nuts and bolts of the Perl language here, but you'll be relieved to learn that it's completely free and widely available. The main resource for reference is **http://www.perl.com**, whilst Matt's Script Archive at **http://worldwidemart.com/scripts** offers a range of foundation scripts to play with, and **http://www.useractive.com** will teach you how to write Perl for yourself. Of course, there have been plenty of books written on the subject, many of which come complete with a CD that may contain useful demonstration software. Run a search on 'Perl' at one of the many online bookshops, such as **http://www.amazon.co.uk/** or **http://www.uk.bol.com/**, to see what's currently available.

ADVANCED: BEEFED-UP BROWSER

Before learning the language, check whether Perl scripts are allowed on the Web server you use to host your site. Generally speaking, if it's a free space service, the answer is no. But if you really think Perl could do wonders for your site, then spending some money on Perl-enabled Web space is well worth the investment. If you're unsure about the benefits of using the scripting language, then it may be worthwhile getting hold of the Windows version of the Apache Web server from **http://www.apache.org/**, and the PC version of Perl from **http://www.perl.com/**. Together these will allow you to turn your PC into a Perl-enabled Web server that will run Perl scripts locally as a testbed.

Plenty of excellent learning resources abound at http://www.useractive.com/, with great material on Perl and CGI

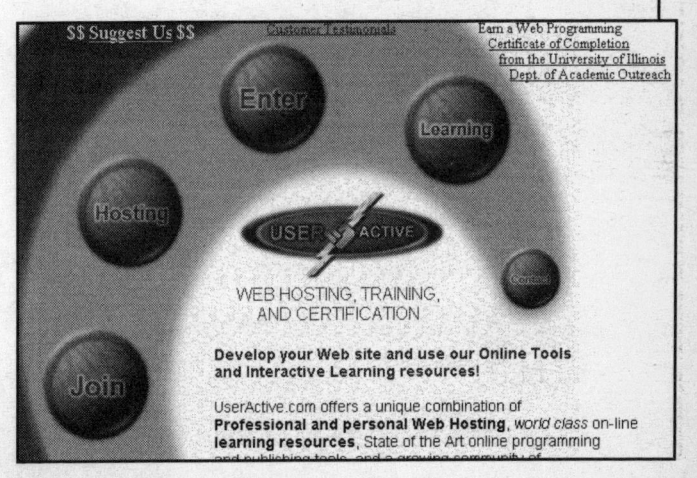

ADVANCED: PLUG-IN POWER

CHAPTER 22

ADVANCED: PLUG-IN POWER

Find out about two of the most popular plug-ins for your Web browser – Apple's QuickTime and Macromedia Flash.

Apple's QuickTime

software is one of its greatest success stories. It is the undisputed Net standard for placing video on Web pages, mainly because it does a better job than anything else in providing high levels of compression whilst retaining top-notch quality. Confidence in QuickTime is almost universal, as demonstrated by the recent release of the online *Star Wars: Episode I* trailer exclusively in this format.

Best of all, QuickTime is not restricted to the great and good of the Web. Most people realise that anybody can download the player software from **http://www.quicktime.apple.com/**. This allows movies to be displayed in your Web browser window.

ADVANCED: PLUG-IN POWER

But it's often thought that creating QuickTime content is the reserve of those who can afford the steep price tags of products like Adobe Premiere. Thanks to a nifty piece of shareware going by the name of QuickEditor, this needn't be the case.

Download the software from **http://wild.ch/quickeditor/** and see for yourself. Everything you need for all but the most advanced movies is possible with this $35 shareware package, including titles, transitions, and audio dubbing. This isn't the place to go into the details of how to use QuickEditor, but look out for a forthcoming tutorial in *Practical Internet's* Home Improvement section. Over the page, you'll find out how to incorporate a QuickTime movie into a Web page.

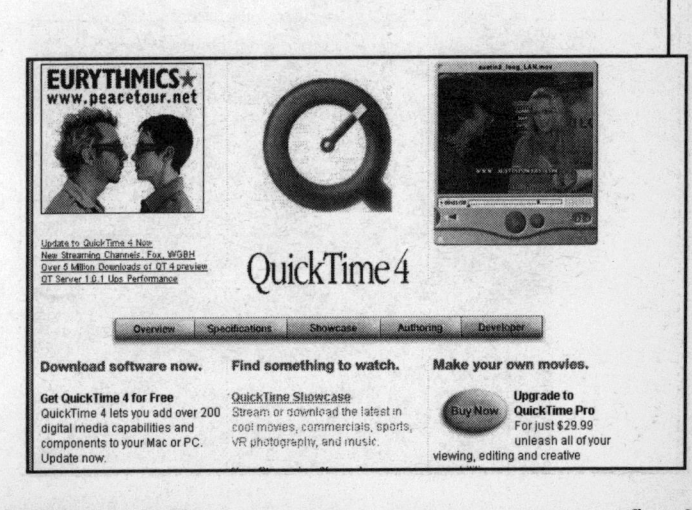

ADVANCED: PLUG-IN POWER

When preparing your QuickTime movie for your Web page, remember to keep its size as small as possible, both in terms of file size and pixel dimension of the movie. The standard QuickTime size of 320 by 240 pixels is ideal. If you're using QuickEditor, you should select to save the movie in a format suitable for streaming across the Net. This means that users will be able to start playing the movie before it has downloaded completely, saving valuable online time. To keep the structure of your Web site tidy, it's a good idea to create a 'movies' directory alongside your 'images' folder. Place all your QuickTime material in this folder.

QuickEditor's main screen shows just how powerful this software can be. Features include AVI/QuickTime conversion, which is useful if you're using a Web camera that produces AVI files

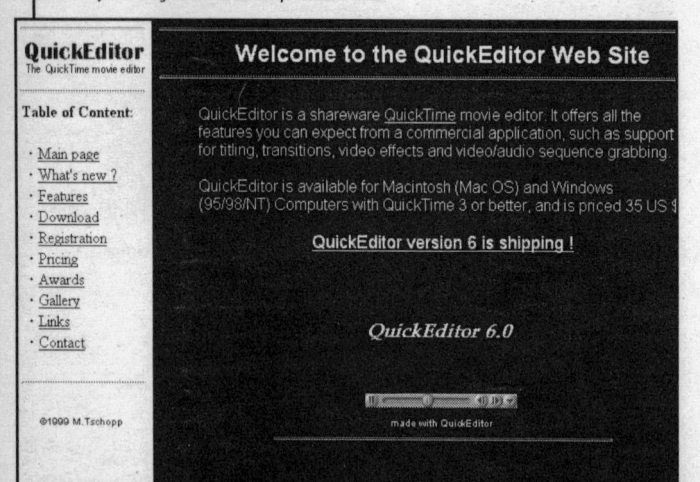

ADVANCED: PLUG-IN POWER

The HTML code for adding a movie is pretty simple. For a 320 by 240 pixel movie, a model tag would be:

```
<EMBED SRC="movies/myflick.mov" AUTOPLAY=TRUE
WIDTH=320 HEIGHT=256 TYPE="video/quicktime"
CONTROLLER=TRUE>
```

The height is given as 256 because the controller bar takes up 16 pixels height in addition to the movie. Autoplay means that the Quicktime plug-in will start to play the movie as soon as enough data has been received to do so. There are dozens of other options for the **EMBED** tag, all of which are listed at the Apple Web site:
http://www.apple.com/quicktime/authoring/embed2.html.

Thanks to QuickTime, you can find out all about the latest weather news without even switching on your television

ADVANCED: PLUG-IN POWER

<u>**Flash**</u> has made a big impact on Web site design since its debut in 1996, and continues to innovate at a rapid pace. For the uninitiated, Flash is a multimedia standard owned by Macromedia which works through a Web browser plug-in. Although the plug-in itself is a free download from **http://www.macromedia.com/**, you need the development software to create Flash media, at a cost of around £199.

Visit the official Macromedia Flash site at http://www.flash.com/ for all the information you could ever need about Flash, plus all of the essential software downloads

ADVANCED: PLUG-IN POWER

Flash is based on vector graphics, meaning that its applets are resizable without losing sharpness. It handles sound, bitmap images, animation, and can work interactively with the user. This interactivity used to be limited to simply clicking a button or setting off an animation by waving the mouse pointer over a sensitive part of the applet. With Flash 4 this has been extended to allow text input, making such applications as chat clients and shopping carts within the reach of people non-programmers.

Pop along to http://www.flasher.net/, one of the few good Flash support sites. Online message boards there are abuzz with suggestions and places to find the best Flash media of the moment

ADVANCED: PLUG-IN POWER

Other enhancements in this version include the ability to incorporate the Net-standard MP3 audio format into Flash applets, allowing much reduced file sizes with complex sound files. Flash applets can also interact with Web server CGI programs and Active Server Pages (ASPs) using GET and POST methods – just like your average HTML form. Better still, Flash applets remember state information, which CGI fanatics will recognise as a major step forward. This basically means that Flash applets can remember the exact state in which they were left, so if you put some items into a Flash shopping cart they will still be there when you look back again on a subsequent visit to the site.

Many mainstream sites are putting Flash to excellent use, such as the vibrant Channel 5 site at http://www.channel5.co.uk/

ADVANCED: PLUG-IN POWER

Aware as ever of the fact that not everybody has a Flash plug-in with their browser, Macromedia have incorporated an advanced Publish function that will also render the applet as an animated (or static) GIF. Scripts to detect whether Flash is being used are included, making integration with old browsers fairly seamless, albeit with a considerable loss of functionality for the user. Animated GIFs can never properly replace Flash applets, especially now that the system is capable of such advanced feats as shopping baskets and text entry.

Overall, there are a number of important improvements to the Flash system in this release. However, the development software still remains beyond the range of the average home page creator, who will be driven to downloading the 30-day trial version of the software to create a few applets for their site, instead of buying the full package.

Macromedia don't just want to sell their product – they want to show off examples of it being put to good use, as their Shockrave pages at http://www.shockrave.com/ demonstrate

CHAPTER 23

ADVANCED: GET READY FOR THE ROBOTS!

ADVANCED: GET READY FOR THE ROBOTS

A common misconception about the Net is that good Web sites automatically become popular. This is simply not true, as all Web sites have to play the publicity game and try to attract visitors using every method possible. However, it is often forgotten that even the most enthusiastic publicity can fail if the site in question lacks 'robot readiness.'

But why should a site aim itself at a robot rather than a real person? Well, the simple fact is that all search engines (sites like Lycos or Infoseek) operate by robotic control. This means that you need to make sure your site is visible to search engines, using various methods.

About.com's articles at http://html.miningco.com/msubmeta.htm reveal all about the mystical Meta tag

ADVANCED: GET READY FOR THE ROBOTS

The best known of all such techniques is the Meta tag, which is a piece of HTML code invisible to the average human user who would be looking at pages using a Web browser. But a robot analysing the HTML will immediately pick up on the Meta tag, and in the case of most search engines will use the keywords and description provided in the tag. Despite popular belief, adding Meta tags is not an ultimate elixir for all your Web site woes. As the tutorial on these pages explains, there's lot more to robot readiness than just Meta tags.

Track down the latest developments and find out how to promote your site successfully at Search Engine Watch (http://www.searchenginewatch.com)

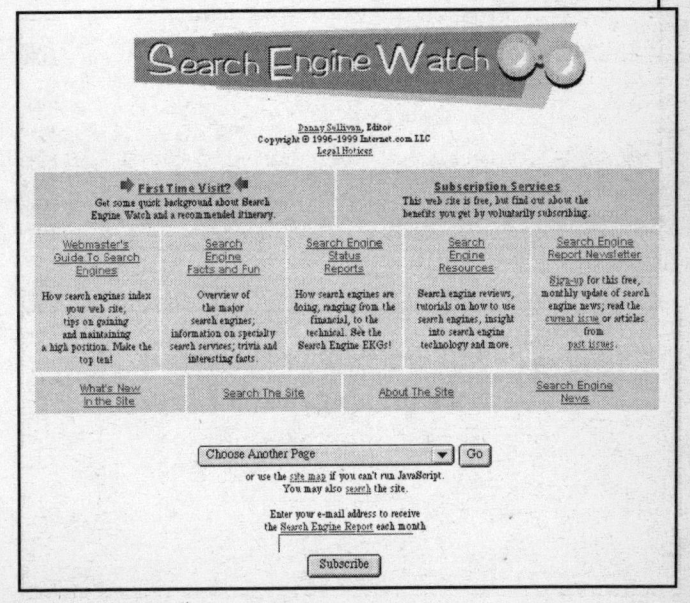

ADVANCED: GET READY FOR THE ROBOTS

By far he most important element of your Web page is its title. Most search engines use it as a key point of reference, so be sure that you include **<TITLE>Put your title here</TITLE>** in every HTML document you create. It should always be the first thing in **<HEAD>** section of the page. Remember that search engines can't 'see' any images on your Web site. To make sure that they still get indexed, be sure to use the **ALT** property of every **IMG** tag in your site. This gives the image a textual description: **<IMG SRC="bessy.gif" ALT="Aunt Bessy's day out at the beach">**

> ALT descriptions also appear when the image can't be loaded

ADVANCED: GET READY FOR THE ROBOTS

Robots simply can't handle imagemaps. As they are often the key to navigating a site, they will exclude search engines from seeing all of your pages. The solution is to always provide standard text links as well as an imagemap, as demonstrated at **http://www.pinet.co.uk/**. It's a great advantage to have all the most important keywords near the top of your HTML document. This might not happen with tables, as shown below. The keywords of the film names look prominent to the human eye, but in terms of HTML code they are near the bottom of the document.

Welcome to dvdreview.net
All the latest DVD news, reviews and special offers

News Updates
- Friends 4 & 5 out in autumn
- Blockbuster Embrace DVD
- South Park Now Out
- Red Dwarf on DVD?
- Where's Star Wars?
- ...and more hot news.

New DVD Reviews
- Lethal Weapon 2
- The Net
- Godzilla
- Tomorrow Never Dies

Hardware Testbed
- Pioneer DVL-919E
- Denon DVD-3000
- Pioneer DV-717
- Yamaha DVD-S700

ADVANCED: GET READY FOR THE ROBOTS

Table problems can be fixed by making sure all the keywords are mentioned in Meta tags, which will be explained shortly. Also, you might consider having a line at the very top of each tabled page with a summary of what's on the page. This is useful for human and robot visitors alike. Frames are yet another popular design element that will wreak havoc with search engine robots. Instead of receiving an index page with lots of links on it, a framed site will start with a short 'frameset' page that will define the dimensions of the different panes.

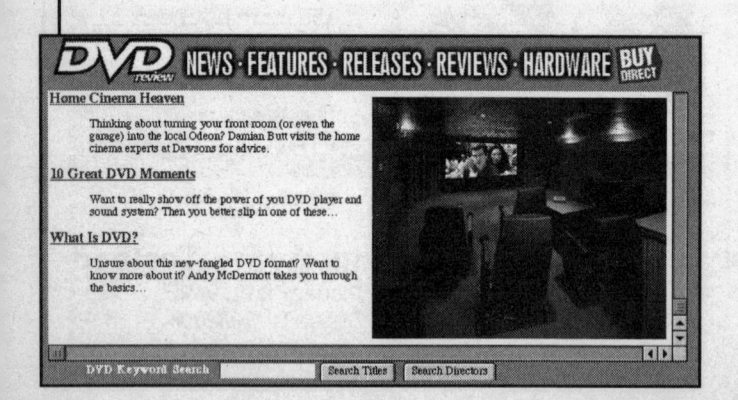

ADVANCED: GET READY FOR THE ROBOTS

Step Six In order to avoid your framed site being ignored by search engines, you need to add Meta tags to the frameset page. Also, use the **<NOFRAMES>** tag after the **<FRAMESET>** tag to give a full description of the site and a list of links to its main pages, as shown above. Now we're finally getting close to putting in those Meta tags. Scribble down a list of keyword phrases – they should each be about two words long. Go to MetaCrawler at **http://www.metacrawler.com**, and run a search on each to see how much competition exists.

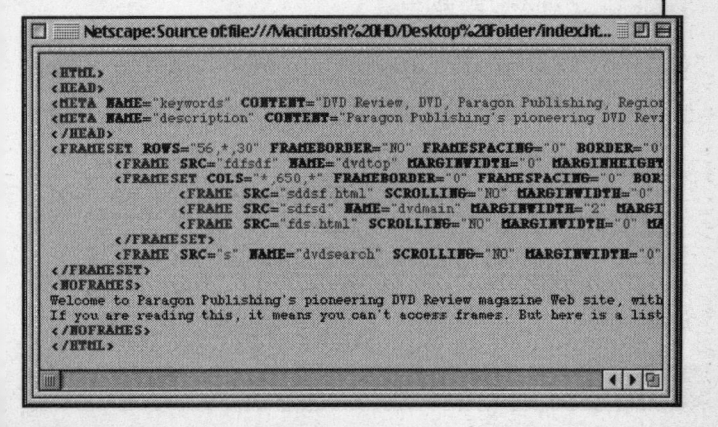

```
<HTML>
<HEAD>
<META NAME="keywords" CONTENT="DVD Review, DVD, Paragon Publishing, Region
<META NAME="description" CONTENT="Paragon Publishing's pioneering DVD Rev
</HEAD>
<FRAMESET ROWS="56,*,30" FRAMEBORDER="NO" FRAMESPACING="0" BORDER="0"
    <FRAME SRC="fdfsdf" NAME="dvdtop" MARGINWIDTH="0" MARGINHEIGHT
    <FRAMESET COLS="*,650,*" FRAMEBORDER="0" FRAMESPACING="0" BOR
        <FRAME SRC="sddsf.html" SCROLLING="NO" MARGINWIDTH="0"
        <FRAME SRC="sdfsd" NAME="dvdmain" MARGINWIDTH="2" MARGI
        <FRAME SRC="fds.html" SCROLLING="NO" MARGINWIDTH="0" MA
    </FRAMESET>
    <FRAME SRC="s" NAME="dvdsearch" SCROLLING="NO" MARGINWIDTH="0"
</FRAMESET>
<NOFRAMES>
Welcome to Paragon Publishing's pioneering DVD Review magazine Web site, with
If you are reading this, it means you can't access frames. But here is a list
</NOFRAMES>
</HTML>
```

ADVANCED: GET READY FOR THE ROBOTS

If your keyword phrases generate thousands of results from Metacrawler, then try to think of keywords that are a little more specific, or take a different angle on the subject matter. It's also a good idea to include both UK and American spelling variations (eg color as well as colour, vacation as well as holiday.) If you're still searching for keywords, visit **http://www.metaspy.com** for inspiration.

When you've got some, create the Meta tag after the **<TITLE>** tag in the main index file of your site:
<META NAME="keywords" CONTENT="keywords,separated,by,commas">.

Do not repeat keywords in an attempt to get a higher ranking – it doesn't work!

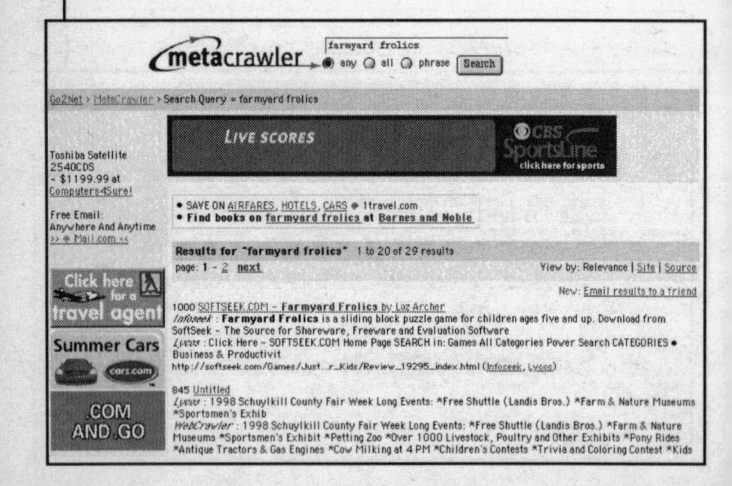

ADVANCED: GET READY FOR THE ROBOTS

The other Meta tag you'll need to create is the description. This is used by some search engines in results pages, as below. It should be longer than 200 characters in length. Make it a concise, attention-grabbing and honest summary of what your site has to offer. Maybe look at competitors' site descriptions before doing yours. Here's an example description tag to adapt:

<META NAME="description" CONTENT= "Description under 200 characters goes here.">

If you want Meta tags on every page, create unique keywords and descriptions for each. When you've finished this, try using a tool like Meta Medic to test them (**http://northernwebs.com/set/setsimjr.html**).

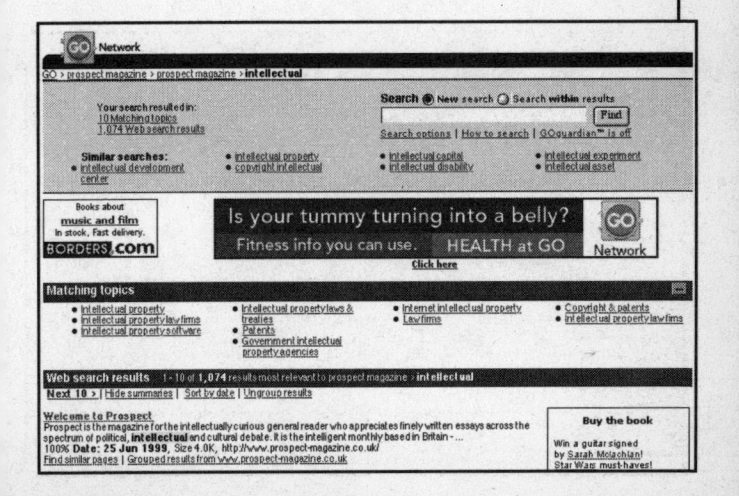

ADVANCED: GET NOTICED

CHAPTER 24

ADVANCED: GET NOTICED

This chapter is full of ideas for promoting your site once it's online, covering everything from Net directories to banner exchanges

One of the most crucial things in promoting your site is to get a listing in Yahoo! (**http://www.yahoo.co.uk/**). This is the original Net directory, which still remains the first port of call for many users. It is also useful for finding the address of a site when only the name is known. Unlike search engines, where sites are automatically indexed by computers, Yahoo! and other Net directories are based on humans trawling the Web and only listing sites worthy of an entry. This means it's also a positive comment on the quality of your site to get a Yahoo! listing.

ADVANCED: GET NOTICED

To get a Yahoo! entry, you need to work out which category would be most suitable for your site to be listed under. Go to the Yahoo! home page and click your way through the menu system until you find the most relevant category. Scroll to the very bottom of the page and click the 'Suggest A Site' link. You'll then need to enter the following information about your site:

1 – Basic Site Information – title, URL, 25 word description.
2 – Category suggestions – list any further suitable categories here.
3 – Contact information – this is kept confidential by Yahoo!
4 – Time Sensitivity – enter dates if your site is temporary.

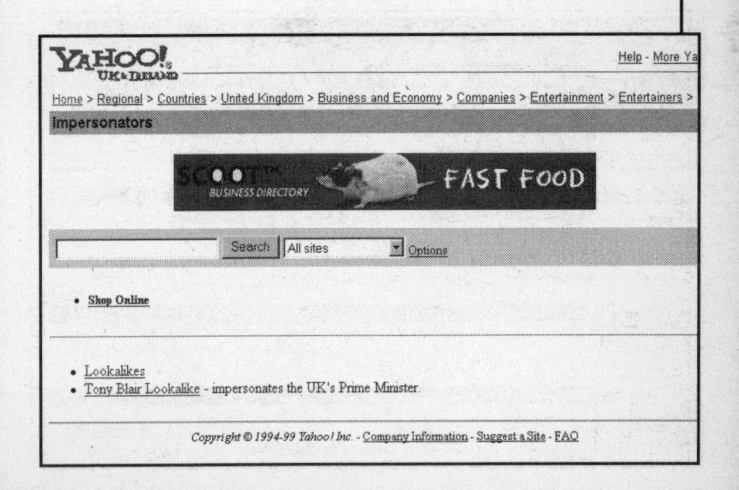

YAHOO!
UK & IRELAND

Help - More Ya

Home > Regional > Countries > United Kingdom > Business and Economy > Companies > Entertainment > Entertainers >
Impersonators

SCOOT BUSINESS DIRECTORY — FAST FOOD

Search | All sites | Options

- Shop Online

- Lookalikes
- Tony Blair Lookalike - impersonates the UK's Prime Minister.

Copyright © 1994-99 Yahoo! Inc. - Company Information - Suggest a Site - FAQ

ADVANCED: GET NOTICED

Search engines are created by computers looking around the Net for sites, and then indexing them with a description and some keywords. It's far from guaranteed that your site's content will properly be reflected if search engines are left to their own devices. Thankfully, help is at hand in the form of Meta tags, which are invisible to the Web site visitor but essential for informing search engines of what your site contains and what it's all about. They're not a magic solution, but with well chosen keywords and a good description they can really make a difference.

Test out your keyword ideas by running a search at http://www.metacrawler.com, to see results from different engines on one page

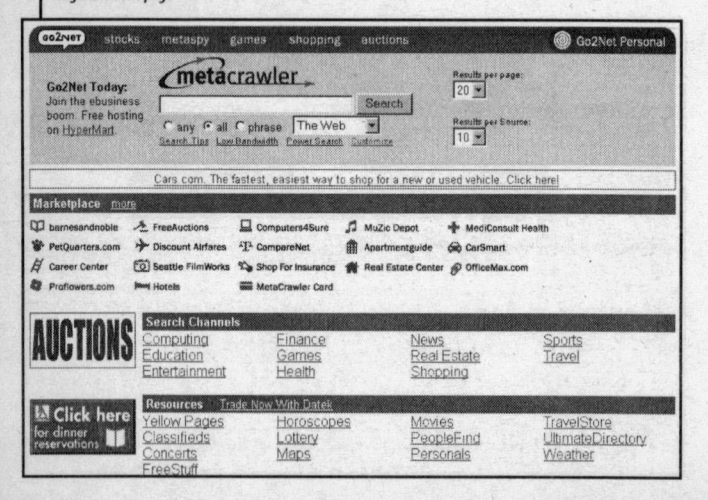

ADVANCED: GET NOTICED

To get some Meta tags of your own, adapt the code below to fit your needs, and then put it just after the **<HEAD>** tag on your Web site's front page. You can also add Meta tags to inside pages, although you should provide unique descriptions and keywords for each page. Keep descriptions under 200 characters and try to limit yourself to only the most relevant keywords; remember to separate keywords with commas.

```
<META NAME="description" CONTENT="Find out all
about farmyard superstar George the Goat here at his
home page, which is packed with four-legged
resources.">
<META NAME="keywords" CONTENT="George the Goat,
farmyard, goat">
```

This free service at http://www.scrubtheweb.com/abs/meta-check.html will take a look at your META tags and figure out whether they could be changed to make your site more likely to appear in search engine results pages

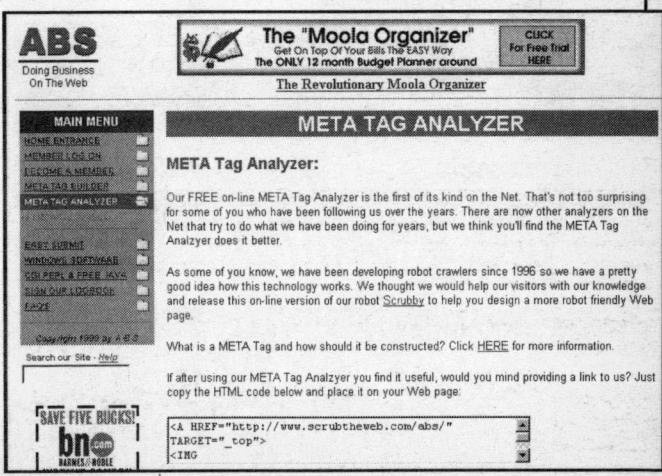

ADVANCED: GET NOTICED

Buzz Building
Hone in on the key aspects of your site – what is really exciting and unique about it. Then target your promotion accordingly. Originality is the key to success on the Net, because people are always keen to visit a site that is offering something different.

Link Liaison
Search engines are crucial to your success. Various services can submit your site to many search engines in one go, saving you a lot of hassle. Most such services cost money, although Submit It at **http://www.submit-it.com/** has a free trial area. Track your success with the Detective at **http://www.did-it.com/**.

This chart shows which search engines Web users claim to have used recently, according to the Tenth GVU Survey. It is crucial to be listed by all of these sites

Yahoo!	90.0%
Alta Vista	81.9%
Excite	69.6%
Lycos	67.0%
Infoseek	63.9%
HotBot	57.0%
WebCrawler	38.5%
MetaCrawler	21.4%
AOL NetFind	17.7%

ADVANCED: GET NOTICED

Banner Barter You don't have to be a big corporation to have a banner advertisement. There's plenty of scope for free advertising through exchange schemes such as LinkExchange at **http://www.linkexchange.com/**. Spend plenty of time creating an eye-catching banner that people can't resist clicking on – look at some successful designs at **http://banner-x-change.net/top10.shtml**.

Usenet Uprising Newsgroups can be a very useful way of letting people know about your site. Usenet is a system made up of subject-classified virtual noticeboards, which can be accessed over the Web at **http://www.deja.com**. Pick out some groups of direct relevance to your site, and tailor a short message to each one.

Banner-X-Change.Net - Top 10 Advertisers

In 468x60 Program

Only members with 500 displays or more are included

Member: HIGHsurf Sites http://members.aol.com/aussie983/home.htm

Click-rate: 4.4%

Member: WebThings http://webthings.hypermart.net

Click-rate: 2.4%

Member: Duckies Place http://home.talkcity.com/JabberWay/duckietoo/enter.html

Click-rate: 1.9%

Member: Make Money! http://www.halyava.ru/igorfil/money.htm

ADVANCED: GET NOTICED

Award Awareness

There is endless potential in the field of Web site awards. Although you would be hard pushed to win one of the well-known awards, there are literally hundreds of others that will get you noticed by featuring your site on their pages. Find out more at Awards Jungle (**http://www.awardsjungle.com**).

Friendly Following

All sites need to encourage loyalty amongst their flock, which involves work on maintaining your pages, through updating and expanding what is on offer. Let people know about what you're doing by setting up a mailing list, using one of these free services **http://www.websitepostoffice.com** or **http://www.listbot.com**.

ADVANCED: GET NOTICED

Memory Maker
Making a site as memorable as possible is another surefire way of getting repeat visitors. Particularly crucial in this field is the URL of your Web site. Most home page URLs are longwinded – probably something like **http://www.geocities.com/Paris/Jardin/1234/**. Get a more memorable one free of charge from CJB (**http://www.cjb.net/**).

Other
ways of making your site one to remember include offering particularly quick access to useful information, or coding your pages efficiently enough to appear in a flash. If you have a commercial site, then regular special offers and other gimmicks such as free delivery work wonders. Don't let promotional efforts overtake the primary aim of providing a useful, up-to-date resource.

CJB.NET
Internet Services
http://www.cjb.net

IS THERE A SERIAL KILLER IN YOUR TOWN? CLICK HERE

| Register Account | Modify Account | Web Mail | Link To Us | Contact Us |

Do you have a web site? Is your web site address too long and hard to remember? Are you looking for a solution, but can't afford your own domain? CJB.NET provides free URL redirection services which allow you to redirect an easy-to-remember *yourname.cjb.net* address to your web site, no matter where it's hosted. CJB.NET offers the following features:

- **No advertisements.** Unlike most other redirection services which place an annoying popup advertisement on your redirect or require a banner or button on your site, CJB.NET has no popups and requires no advertising on your site.

- **Subdomain address.** Some services offer redirection using a folder under their domain, but with CJB.NET, you get your very own *yourname.cjb.net* subdomain address.

- **Path forwarding.** With path forwarding, you can link to images, files, and subdirectories on your site through your CJB.NET address.

- **URL hiding.** With the Hide URL option, your CJB.NET address will be displayed in the location bar of your browser, thus "hiding" your real web site address. People bookmarking your site will bookmark your CJB.NET address, and search engines will index your site using your CJB.NET address.

- **Web mail.** Each URL redirection account includes a corresponding web mail account that receives mail sent to any @username.cjb.net address. This allows you to use professional webmaster@ and sales@ addresses along with your CJB.NET subdomain, or any other addresses that match the theme of your site.

- **Domain redirection.** Optional domain redirection services, which allow you to redirect your own .com, .net, or .org domain to your site, are available through redirection.net for a low one-time $30.00 setup fee.

Registering your new CJB.NET address is fast, easy, and, best of all, completely free. Your new CJB.NET address will be activated immediately upon registration, and you can modify it instantly at any time. Don't let someone else register the CJB.NET address you want, sign up now!

Please note that warez sites, porn sites, illegal MP3 sites, or any other sites that promote or are otherwise involved in any kind of illegal activities may not use this service and will have their accounts terminated if found or reported.

CHAPTER 25

APPENDIX: 32 TOP TIPS 105 HOT SITES

APPENDIX: 32 TOP TIPS/105 HOT SITES

- Test out the most effective use of JPEG compression for yourself by taking the image and converting it into JPEGs at different compression levels.

- If you're tired of paying good money for more computer books, Jeffrey Zeldman offers to answer web design questions at **http://www.zeldman.com**.

- Remember the 30 second rule: if your page hasn't displayed within this time, you're liable to lose visitors. This means that a page totalling more than 90k in size (HTML and graphics) will be too slow.

- Supply a link on each page to let visitors send you email. Use the 'mailto' method in HTML, for example **<A HREF = "mailto:james@paragon.co.uk">Email me feedback</A>** would create a link to my email address.

Big Nose Bird
http://www.bignosebird.com
"Everything you need to build great sites."

GIF Lube
http://www.giflube.com
Clean up your act, cut down the file size.

Hitometer Free
http://www.hitometer.com
Find out how many visitors you're getting.

Inside the Web
http://www.insidetheweb.com
Get a free interactive message board.

Made Easy Network
http://made-easy.net
Help for PC and Net beginners.

Media Builder
http://www.mediabuilder.com
Jazz up your site with flashy media.

MP3.com
http://www.mp3.com
Activate your site with MPEG3.

Web Developer
http://www.webdeveloper.com
All the latest Web development news.

WebMonkey
http://www.webmonkey.com
HotWired's top-notch Web design site.

Web Site Journal
http://www.websitejournal.com
News and views for Web designers.

Website Post Office
http://www.websitepostoffice.com
A free mailing list for your site.

Allaire HomeSite
http://www.allaire.com/Products/HomeSite
Find out more about this Web editing software.

APPENDIX: 32 TOP TIPS/105 HOT SITES

- Brush up on your Web graphics at **http://www.unplug.com/great/graphics.htm**. It's full of handy hints and tips.

- Check how many people visit your site with a free page counter from **http://www.pagecount.com**.

- Make sure any background image you use doesn't clash with your text. There's nothing more annoying than not being able to read what's written on a Web page.

- Copyright laws apply to the Net, too – don't rip off other sites' material.

HotMetal
http://www.softquad.com
Grab hold of some great editing software.

SiteOwner
http://www.siteowner.com/
Quick access to LinkExchange tools.

CJB Net
http://www.cjb.net/
Get a snappy URL for your site.

Colour Palette Map
http://www.the-light.com/colclick.html
Cruise through Web safe colours in no time.

iSyndicate
http://www.isyndicate.com
News headlines for free on your site!

did-it Detective
http://www.did-it.com/
Track down your search engine ranking.

Frames and search engines
http://www.searchenginewatch.com/webmasters/frames.html
Find out how to mix the two on this page.

Informatik
http://www.informatik.com
Get WebParse software here (to decode form output.)

Response-o-Matic
http://www.response-o-matic.com/
Forms on your site without a script in sight.

Microsoft Typography
http://www.microsoft.com/typography/fontpack
Grab yourself some free Web-friendly fonts.

Wacky.org
http://www.wacky.org/fonts
Snazzy fonts from a trendy site.

Blue Vinyl Fonts
http://www.reflectdesign.com/bvfonts
Homegrown fonts in Windows TrueType format only.

Build a Web Site in 24 Hours   Chapter 25

APPENDIX: 32 TOP TIPS/105 HOT SITES

- Always use a plain background on your home page. Patterns can render text illegible.

- Don't spend a fortune on books about Web design. The best resources are online – see **http://www.htmlgoodies.com/**.

- Avoid using background music on your site. It wastes bandwidth and normally sounds awful.

- If you like the look of a site, then select 'View source' in your browser and see how it's done.

- Think carefully about how much personal information you put on your home page. Certainly avoid disclosing your address and phone number, for simple reasons of personal security.

Sassy Fonts
http://www.trashed.org/sassyfonts
Funky, Distressed and Dingbats fonts

wonderweb
http://www.wonderweb.net/typo/index.htm
Font fishing fun in French.

Fontaholics Anonymous
http://www.flash.net/~fontahol
Mac users: grab hold of TTConvertor here.

Astigmatic One Eye Foundry
http://www.astigmatic.com/aoeff/freefonts.html
Fuel your design ideas with this modest collection.

Letraset Ripper
http://www.esselte.com/ripper/index.html
The ultimate Try Before You Buy font site.

Truetype Typography
http://www.truetype.demon.co.uk
Find out more about TrueType technology.

007 Fonts
http://www.007fonts.com
Hundreds of Windows-only fonts.

Emerald City Fontworks
http://www.speakeasy.org/~ecf
Spanky's Bungalow and many more fonts on offer.

Chank Free Fonts
http://www.chank.com/freefonts.html
Home site of the undisputed font king.

Opera Software
http://www.operasoftware.com
Opera: a HTML compliant Web browser.

BareBones Software
http://www.barebones.com
Makers of the ultimate Mac text editor.

Website Garage
http://www.websitegarage.com
Run your site in for a quick MOT.

APPENDIX: 32 TOP TIPS/105 HOT SITES

- Jazz up your table designs by applying background textures or images to them. Just add a **BACKGROUND** attribute to the **TABLE**, **TR** or **TD** tag of your choice. Of course, background colours can also be applied by using **BGCOLOR** instead

- RankThis at **http://www.rankthis.com** is a nifty tool that will tell you how highly your site is listed in 10 key search engines, based on keywords that you specify. If your site isn't listed at all, then you can take a look at the competition and work out how to do better

- Get some cash by putting banner adverts on your site. Take a look at **http://www.safe-audit.com** and **http://www.clickagents.com** and pick some adverts relevant to your home page.

WebMonkey Tutorials by Thau
http://www.hotwired.com/webmonkey/javascript/tutorials/tutorial1.html
How JavaScript really should be done.

Voodoo
http://rummelplatz.uni-mannheim.de/~skoch/js/script.htm
Twelve individual tutorials teach JavaScript from the ground up.

HotSyte
http://www.serve.com/hotsyte
All JavaScript life is here.

Developer Central
http://developer.netscape.com/tech/javascript
From the people who brought you Javascript...

Java Goodies
http://www.javagoodies.com
Jo Burns' ultimate Java tutorial site.

Ask a Pro
http://www.inquiry.com/techtips/js-pro
Have yourJavaScript woes solved by a 'pro'

ECMA Script Spec
http://www.ecma.ch/stand/ecma-262.htm
The latest and greatest scripting standard.

Builder SuperScripter
http://www.builder.com/Programming/Kahn
The finest JavaScript tools on the planet.

Javascript Source
http://javascript.internet.com
Everything from cookies to backgrounds.

scripts.co.uk
http://www.scripts.co.uk
Impressive searchable resource site.

Dynamic IT
http://javascript.connect-2.co.uk
Find out more about linking DHTML and Javascript.

JSWorld.com
http://www.jsworld.com
News and feature-led scripting site.

- Recent studies show that the average Net user only scrolls down on 25 per cent of Web pages they visit. The moral of this tale is to make sure that the top part of your pages are eye-catching and contain decent navigational links.

- While it's a good idea to keep graphics small in file size, there are times when large downloads may be required – for example, with detailed or simply enormous images. In this case, give your users a helping hand by making the size of large files clear before downloading has begun.

- Try to design your Web pages so they display well on an 800 x 600 resolution screen. You can find out what resolution your screen is running at from the Windows Control Panel or the Monitors and Sound Control Panel on Macs.

MailStart
http://www.mailstart.com/form
Let your visitors check their email on your site.

HTML Writers' Guild
http://www.hwg.org/
Webweavers of the world unite!

GIF Wizard
http://www.gifwizard.com
Jazz up your GIF files free of charge.

Web Pages That Suck
http://www.webpagestsuck.com
How low can Web design go?

Fork In The Head
http://www.forkinthehead.com
Let bad sites know just how awful they are.

CuteHTML
http://www.globalscape.com
Great new text editor for HTML files.

ProjectCool
http://www.projectcool.com/
Excellent Web design reference site.

Pretty HTML
http://mpp.at/pretty
Automatically tidy up your HTML coding.

EyeDropper
http://www.inetia.com/eyedropperEng.asp
Find out the colour code for any pixel on your screen.

BrowserMaster
http://www.vasile.com/racecar/stampware
Find out how your Web page looks on different monitor sizes.

JPEG Optimizer
http://www.xat.com
Get the compression/quality balance right.

2002 Background Sounds & Images
http://www.austech.com
Plenty of top quality clip media for your site.

APPENDIX: 32 TOP TIPS/105 HOT SITES

- Remember that HTML tables can have background images and colours specified in the same way as the **<BODY>** tag of any page. Simply add **BGCOLOR** or **BACKGROUND** properties to the **<TABLE>**, **<TR>** or **<TD>** tags as required.

- If your Web pages feature lots of links or complicated forms, then use the **TABINDEX** to specify the order in which a set of links, or form elements, should be highlighted when the user presses the 'tab' key repeatedly. Basically, add **TABINDEX="1", TABINDEX="2"** and so on to the **<A HREF>** tag for link ordering, or the **<INPUT>** tags for form ordering.

- Make your own Tool Tip pop-up messages with the **ACRONYM** tag. The code **<ACRONYM="What You See Is What You Get">WYSIWYG</ACRONYM>** is all that is needed.

Apache Web server
http://www.apache.org/dist/binaries/win32
Test your CGI scripts offline with this server.

LiveImage
http://www.mediatec.com
Automatically generate imagemaps.

WebForms
http://www.q-d.com
Software tool for easy form generation.

Home page control
http://www.4developers.com/homepage
Reconfigure browser home pages with a button click.

UnMozify
http://www.evolve.co.uk
Relive past Web browsing offline.

SiteSweeper
http://www.sitetech.com
Check your site for broken links.

ICQ Panel
http://www.icq.com/panels
Add an ICQ button panel to your site.

TechMailings
http://www.techmailings.com
Subscribe to a technology mailing list.

Guestbook
http://www.guestbook.com
Get a free guestbook for your site.

Associate Programs
http://www.associateprograms.com
Earn some cash from your site with an affiliate scheme.

World Wide Web Consortium
http://www.w3.org/
The official line on everything Web related.

HTML Tutorials for the Complete Idiot
http://www.geocities.com/SiliconValley/Campus/1924
Enough said.

- Eight out of 10 Web surfers say that they use search engines as the first step in finding a site. To make sure that you get found, you need to submit your site to at least **http://www.altavista.com**, **http://www.excite.co.uk**, **http://www.hotbot.com**, **http://www.infoseek.com**, and **http://www.lycos.com**.

- An eMarketer (**http://www.emarketer.com**) survey suggests that Web users are increasingly lacking in patience in the download time stakes. 49 per cent will give up waiting if your page takes longer than fifteen seconds to load, and only five per cent will wait for pages that still haven't fully appeared after thirty seconds!

- If your home page URL is long or difficult to remember, then you'll love the free service on offer at **http://www.cjb.net**. You can create your own subdomain (eg **http://mypage.cjb.net**) that forwards users to your existing URL. Better still, it is advert free.

ArtToday
http://www.arttoday.com
Fee-paying clip art and font service.

Animated GIF of the day
http://www.mediabuilder.com/graphicsagifday.html
Bask in the animated glory of a different GIF every day.

Clipart.com
http://www.clipart.com
More free graphics than the mind can imagine.

Tweety Pie's Clipart Connection
http://www.ltexpress.com/ndxbox1.html
Cartoon clip art and a whole lot more.

Inki's Clipart
http://www.inki.com/clipart
Funky modern clip art for the discerning site designer.

Binaries.org
http://www.binaries.org/graphics.html
Find design inspiration here by looking at others' work.

Barry's Clipart Server
http://www.barrysclipart.com
Excellent animated GIFs, average static graphics.

Railroad Clipart
http://www.ribbonrail.com/art
Clip art for the rail enthusiast.

WebPlaces Search
http://www.webplaces.com/search
Search the Web for graphic files.

Zidelli Graphics
http://www.geocities.com/SouthBeach/2177/graphics.html
Navigation-oriented free graphic selection.

Alex's Animated GIF Shop
http://www.wsdaents.com
Generous free selection, option to pay for more.

Animation Factory
http://www.animfactory.com
Goldmine of free images (non-commercial use only.)

APPENDIX: 32 TOP TIPS/105 HOT SITES

- Never change the size of an image by altering the **WIDTH** and **HEIGHT** properties of an **IMG** tag. Enlarging images make them look awful, whilst reducing them wastes bandwidth. Simply alter the size of the graphic itself instead.

- Don't provide a link that goes outside your site without making it clear where it will take the visitor, and why you are sending them away from your pages. Otherwise you'll both confuse and lose visitors in one easy step.

- Almost every Web space provider on the Net compared: HostIndex at **http://www.hostindex.com**.

ZapZone Networks
http://www.zzn.com
Create your own Web-based email service.

HTMLTidy
http://www.w3.org/People/Raggett/tidy
Clean up your HTML coding act.

WebCompiler
http://www.webcompiler.com
Compile your Web site onto a floppy disk.

Matt's Script Archive
http://worldwidemart.com/scripts
The ultimate online scripting resource.

UserActive
http://www.useractive.com
Web technology learning resource.

Beyond the Bones of HTML
http://www.avalon.net/~librarian/bones
Venture into the realm of advanced HTML coding.

ebGate lite
http://www.ebutterfly.com/eb/ebgate.html
Javascript-based tool to password-protect your site.

efuse
http://www.efuse.com/
Dan Will-Harris' five-step site making solution.

Excite Affiliates Network
http://affiliate.excite.com
Make money for carrying Excite content on your site.

Impressionz
http://www.impressionz.co.uk
Three different banner exchange networks. One site.

UK Banners
http://www.ukbanners.com/
500 free banner impressions for new users.

UK Buttons
http://www.ukbuttons.com/
The baby brother of UK Banners.